Second Edition

THE INSTANT MARKETING PLAN

How to Create a
Money Grabbing Marketing Plan in
Just One Day!

by Mark Nolan

PUMA PUBLISHING COMPANY
Santa Maria, California
1998

Library of Congress Cataloging-in-Publication Data

Nolan, Mark, 1958-
    The instant marketing plan : how to create a money grabbing
marketing plan in just one day / by Mark Nolan. -- 2nd ed.
        p.   cm.
    Includes index.
    ISBN 0-940673-57-6
    1. Marketing--Planning.   I. Title.
HF5415.13.N64   1998
    658.8'02--dc21   98-18940
                                                         CIP

ABOUT THE AUTHOR

Author Mark Nolan has owned and successfully operated an advertising agency and several other businesses. He's listed in *Who's Who in Advertising*. Nolan presents personal and behind-the-scenes information and expertise drawing on his experiences in his advertising agency and as consultant to a wide variety of businesses. He offers case histories of a wide range of businesses which have used new or improved marketing plans to accomplish turnarounds and/or quick sales increases.

Nolan dispels many popular misconceptions which have made marketing seem a confusing and strange endeavor. He shows that there is no mystery to good marketing and explains the foundations of successful strategy in an easy-to-understand format. Nolan wrote this book for folks who need results *today*. It doesn't deal with theory; it focuses on what works and is successful in the real world of business and marketing. He presents the information with humor and anecdotes in a relaxed, conversational style of writing. We are confident that you will heartily agree.

TABLE OF CONTENTS

ACKNOWLEDGEMENTS

This book would not have been possible without the extraordinary assistance of Curt Scott of Crown Publishing Company. He never ceases to amaze us with his dedication to producing an excellent product. Considerable credit is due to Ken Korczak who organized a three-foot-high stack of miscellaneous material into a manageable manscript. Louise Turner provided outstanding support editing the early (and often incomprehensible) drafts. Thanks, as usual, to Dan Poynter of Para Publishing for his invaluable advice.

PREFACE

Injecting *Method* into your Marketing

You don't need a college degree in marketing to create your own successful marketing plan. You don't need years of experience, an MBA or a high-priced consultant ...

... this book is all you need.

The Instant Marketing Plan is designed to help you achieve business success and make a lot of money by showing you an easy, *step-by-step* way to turn your business enterprise into a high-powered, wealth-generating success.

That's a bold promise, and we don't make it lightly. We make the promise because we know that this book delivers. *The Instant Marketing Plan* helps you to accomplish your mission in several ways:

First, one of the secrets of developing an excellent strategy to sell your products or service, is knowing what questions to ask about your business: questions that specifically answer, what? how? when? why? where?

But you'll find that we do more than merely ask you questions. We'll guide you through finding the right answers. This book moves you toward organizing your answers in a way that develops a foundation that will become the basis of a marketing plan tailored for your business.

Next, *The Instant Marketing Plan* helps you put the steps of your personal marketing strategy into a logical order of priority based upon how each step relates to your business. Then, it helps you to tie everything together in a simple and clear, comprehensive plan, complete with a "to do" checklist, and more.

By the time you make your way to the final chapter, you will clearly

You don't need an MBA or a high-priced consultant.

understand and identify your marketing goals, and you will have a straightforward, solid, written marketing that will help you reach the highest level of business success your hard work will allow.

All this, and we expect to have some fun along the way! We don't intend to bore you with a college textbook–style lecture or pages of gray, droning copy and statistics. Our author's approach is decidedly lively, punchy, to-the-point; we believe that to be truly successful, you have to thoroughly enjoy what you do. *The Instant Marketing Plan* is designed to bring you both enjoyment and business success.

Chapter 1

Your Marketing Plan: Don't Leave Home without it

Why do some businesses fail while others succeed?

Jay Conrad Levinson, in his fine book, *Guerrilla Marketing*, put it this way:

"In order to engage in successful marketing, you absolutely must start out with a marketing plan. Rest assured, the difference between many a success and failure is market planning and nothing else."

Most businesses don't plan to fail. They simply fail to plan. Why is market planning so crucial? It connects you with your customers. The most important part of your business enterprise are your customers! Without customers you don't have a business—you have a *hobby*.

Would you build a house without a building plan? Would you go into a big football face-off without a game plan? Would you travel on business without a travel plan?

I think not! Yet most businesses—most business owners—fail to prepare any marketing plan at all. They fly blind and hope for "good fortune." But the fact is, success seldom happens by luck.

How and where do you plan to get customers for your business?

Most business don't plan to fail. They simply fail to plan.

Most business owners answer, "I don't know." Remember the movie *Field of Dreams*? Remember that preposterous baseball park in the middle of a cornfield? Actor Kevin Costner is told by some mystical voice, *"If you build it, they will come."* Well, many business owners appear to rely upon help from ... er, mystical sources, I guess.

In fact, many otherwise intelligent business persons harbor the idea that when they open their doors for business, the customers will just happen by and spend their money! Unfortunately for the average small business owner, he (or she) spends more time planning his family's vacation than planning the marketing strategy that may make or break his business. No wonder many businesses fail! To succeed in business, you must have plenty of customers and cash flow. Both are generated by following a marketing plan step-by-step.

A carefully-prepared marketing plan may require weeks to map out, and can fill dozens of pages, complete with text, charts, graphs and projections of all varieties. But before I overwhelm anyone, you should know that there is something to be said for simplicity. A marketing plan does not necessarily take weeks of sweat and paper sifting. In fact, being too ambitious at first can stop you before you even start. Toward that end, we have put together just the thing you need to jump-start your enterprise—

A One-Day Marketing Plan!

No, it's not a get-rich-quick scheme or hasty bailing-wire-and-bubble gum program. *The One Day Marketing Plan* is designed to be a simple, organized way for you to put your creative thoughts in order, and to get you off of your... *Square One*. The plan will help you start making money right away with your merchandise or service—but it also provides you with flexibility to make refinements in your marketing strategy as you proceed. The important thing is to get started! The Chinese poet Lau Tzu said: *"The journey of a thousand miles begins with a single step."* Come along with us. We'll help you take that first step right now!

Okay. Let's say you are starting a new business. You have a lot of things to think about, but which one of those things is the most important?

↓ Cash Flow ↑

Listen to what C.D. Peterson said recently in *Success Magazine*:

"To achieve financial freedom, you need customers and cash flow. Rather, you need paying customers and positive cash flow; lots of paying customers and positive cash flow; a mob of paying customers and a raging river of positive cash flow."

Obvious? Of course. Cash flow is the lifeblood of your business. Whether you're just starting out in business or you're an old fox, cash flow determines the health of your venture.

Healthy cash flow can bring astounding success to a new business. It can boost an adolescent business into thriving maturity and rescue a struggling business from the brink of disaster.

On the other hand, even the richest, most successful entrepreneurs can have cash shortages at times. A sudden, unforeseen shortage of cash flow can strangle even established, respected business establishments. In fact, it happened to me—twice!

"The journey of a thousand miles begins with a single step."

And look at what happened to Donald Trump. Remember when Chrysler had to go to the government on bended knee and ask for a special loan?

Yes, cash flow is important. *All important!* To get cash flow you need—you guessed it!—SALES! Cash flow comes from sales. This doesn't mean you must personally go out and knock on doors and become a salesman. I've done that. It's not much fun.

Your goal is to trade something of value to other people in exchange for something else of value (their money). You may do this in a host of different ways, often by "remote control." But you *must* have a plan!

You must have a plan!

Throughout this book we refer to your "product." Your product may be anything produced as a result of manufacturing, agriculture, intellectual creativity (books, videotapes, display ads, multimedia presentations, modern art, *etc.*), skills or services.

If your product falls into the general category of services, your primary promotion techniques will probably be variations of direct marketing. These may include direct mail, classified ads, *Yellow Pages* advertising, word-of-mouth, display ads, broadcast (radio/TV) commercials, package stuffers, matchbooks, press releases and telephone solicitation.

If your product falls into the general category of a commodity (goods, *etc.*), you have at your disposal a greater variety of methods to promote your business. In addition to the techniques describe above, the first two cash-flow leveraging techniques described below can be powerful tools.

Cash-flow leveraging technique #1:
Let Others Sell The Product And Pay You A Royalty

You can authorize someone else to do most of the sales work and simply pay you a small royalty on each sale. This is how inventors and book authors often "sell" their products.

A 79-years–young friend of mine, Woody Hall, has dozens of crazy novelty product ideas on the market that are paying him royalties. He grants manufacturers the rights to these product ideas, and the manufacturers do all the selling and send him 5% of the gross income. If you have "a better idea for a mousetrap" and that way of doing business appeals to you, you should read Woody's book, *Your Ideas Could Be Worth a Fortune.*

How hard is it to come up with an idea that sells? Woody simply looks at a popular item and asks questions such as, "What if it were bigger? Smaller? Flat? Square? Round?" For example, when the happy face buttons and stickers were all the rage, Woody asked himself, *"What if it were round?"* He spent one afternoon "working" on the idea. He took a ping pong ball, painted it yellow, drew a happy face on it and sent it to a manufacturer along with a special submission form he created which protects his ideas. The company promptly sold 3 million of them—and paid Woody 5%. Dumb luck? Doesn't look like it—he has over 147 similar offbeat ideas on the market. This is a fun way to make extra cash flow. It's not as fast as some methods you'll learn about in later chapters, but it's very easy "work" if you enjoy it.

Richard Bach is the author of the book *Jonathan Livingston Seagull*. He turned in his manuscript to the publisher and went on vacation, barnstorming his biplane across the Midwest. One day a few months later, he called his publisher just to check in. They asked him to get to New York immediately. His book was #1 on the bestseller list. He was wanted on the television talk show circuit.

Oh, and by the way, there was over a million dollars in his royalty account, and where should they send his check?

The publisher and bookstores did all the selling for Bach. They also kept 90% of the money. But so what? While he was flying and having fun, they were manufacturing and selling his books. I'm sure he felt a million dollars was a fair royalty. Wouldn't you?

Jonathan Livingston Seagull is a great little book, by the way, for people interested in freedom. Here's a quote from it that I read when I need an attitude adjustment:

"What he had once hoped for the Flock, he now gained for himself alone; he learned to fly, and was not sorry for the price he had paid. Jonathan Seagull discovered that boredom and fear and anger are the reasons that a gull's life is so short, and with these gone from his thought, he lived a long, fine life indeed."

Cash-flow leveraging technique #2: Wholesale Your Product

To Retailers

You can sell wholesale to retail stores and/or mail-order catalog companies and let them sell the product to the public for you.

To sell to mail-order catalogs, you need to fill out an information page known as the Merchandise Data Sheet. Send it along with a sample ad or blurb on the item and a photo or even a sample. Mail it to the catalog company to the attention of the Merchandising Director. They're pretty good about taking time to look at almost any product. They have regular meetings to look over new products to include in their upcoming catalogs. They may send you more forms to fill out to get more specific facts from you.

The good news is that if they do put your item in their catalogs it can sell like crazy! They buy by the pallet load. Even if the product bombs by their standards, they will need hundreds or thousands of your item just to fill the orders they do get. And if it takes off—look out! Their millions of customers can buy trainloads of products in short order.

I helped a client to sell 500,000 units of his product—wholesale—to mail-order companies. He came up with the idea of taking little two-inch pieces of rubber tubing sealed on one end, and using them to replace the coating on dishwasher prongs. All automatic dishwashers have racks for cups with steel prongs covered with a rubber coating. The coating can come off after a few years and the steel prongs can scratch your dishes and drip rust into the machine.

What do you do? The dishwasher still works—the only problem is with the prongs. Now, thanks to my friend, for a few dollars you can slip these little rubber tubes over the prongs—and they're as good as new!

He sent the catalog companies a sales letter and a sample ad for the item. A few of the companies put them right into their new catalogs. Soon after the item showed up in a few of the catalogs, many of the remaining companies saw it and jumped on the bandwagon, too. They seem to copy each other.

A friend of mine sells wristwatches with pictures of various dogs on the faces. Those watches are among the top five best-selling products in several catalogs right now. He doesn't manufacture them—he imports them from Asia, wholesales them to catalog companies, and lets them do all of the selling for him.

Cash-flow leveraging technique #3: Hire Sales People On Straight Commission To Sell for You

Another leveraged selling method is to hire people to go out and sell for you and pay them a commission. Run an exciting ad in the classifieds under "sales help wanted," and you'll often be stunned by the response. There are plenty of sales people out there looking for a hot product to sell. You could have one, ten, or a hundred or more sales people working for you. Put them on straight commission. Pay them for only what they sell—a percentage of the cash flow they bring in. This is a powerful way to duplicate you own efforts through the efforts of other people. Just remember, it's a big challenge and can be a lot of hard work to manage a sales force.

Cash-flow leveraging technique #4:
Sell By "Remote Control"

With Scientific Advertising!

In my opinion, the very best way for you to sell is to use scientific advertising. That's what I do. I let the advertisement act as my "salesman in print." It works for me day and night— and I am free to run my business! And it can work for you, too!

Relax! I won't tell you to run out and spend a fortune on advertising that may or may not work. Instead, I'll show you how to start smart by getting free coverage in magazines and newspapers. Yes, free! It's far easier than you might think.

Don't worry if you've never done this before and don't know how. I'll teach you what I've learned about it right here and now. If you do it my way, you'll discover not only that it's simple to do, but that it can be a lot of fun and make a lot of money for you.

Albert Einstein once wrote, *"If I had my life to live over again, I would elect to be a trader of goods rather than a student of science. I think barter is a noble thing. I need to know more about it."*

No kidding! We all need to know more about it. If you learned to walk, talk, ride a bike, read a book. and drive a car—you can learn to make money with the methods you're learning from this book. Virtually anyone can do this. It will work—if you work.

Yes, selling a product or service can pay you a nice income, but money isn't enough by itself. You also need the freedom and free time to enjoy your new-found prosperity.

The very best way for you to sell is to use scientific advertising.

To gain true financial freedom, you must be able to turn on the cash flow just as you'd turn on a faucet and make the cash flow whenever you need it.

So what's the rest of the secret?

The way to make a lot of money without getting stuck on the treadmill in the rat race is by using the principle of cash flow in combination with the principle of—LEVERAGE!

I don't mean financial debt leverage, as in borrowing and investing. Being in debt is not financial freedom. I mean leverage of your time.

You may have heard a business owner say, *"I'm working sixteen hours a day for myself so I don't have to work eight hours a day for someone else."* You may have said it yourself.

And it's true. Many business owners work twice as hard for twice as many hours to earn the same pay they could in half the time working for someone else.

That's not financial freedom! That's being caught in the rat race. As Lily Tomlin said, *"What's the point in 'winning' the race if you become a rat in the process?"*

You need leverage of your time and leverage of your energy and leverage of your marketing—so you get ten times as much in results and income with only one-tenth the investment of time effort and money.

Isn't that what you really want? To make a lot more money while doing a lot less work? Now you can.

"What's the point in 'winning' the the race if you become a rat in the process?"

CASH FLOW + LEVERAGE = FINANCIAL FREEDOM

Remember what I said at the beginning of this chapter? Customers bring in the sales and cash flow. But what brings in the customers? Marketing. Not just haphazard marketing—planned marketing.

Marketing must follow a plan.

Cash flow, leverage, and financial freedom—all this begins with a sound marketing plan. In the next chapter, I will walk you through the process of analyzing your business and creating a tailored-for-your-business marketing plan…step-by-step.

Chapter 2

A basic marketing plan in just one day

To develop your one-day basic plan, just answer the questions which follow, then proceed to implement your Instant Marketing Plan at the end of this chapter. Right now, don't worry about those questions that require more than just your in-house research; just mark them for follow-up. During the refining stage of the plan development, you can later modify your Instant Marketing Plan as required.

Your answers to the questions and your Instant Marketing Plan should be documented, so put them on paper (or into your word processor). Putting everything down in black-and-white provides you with the remarkable advantage of seeing the big picture, and helps you to uncover new thoughts or directions for your business.

To begin with, don't worry about form, writing style or anything else. We'll get to that later. Right now you just need to get started. Got your paper and pencils? Okay, let's begin!

Title Page

Page one of your marketing plan is merely a cover page. It's a small detail, but empires are built on small details. We might as well be detail-oriented from the beginning. The cover page will include your company name, the date of your last revision, and a statement of confidentiality. The next page is an example.

> *Putting everything down in black-and-white provides you with the remarkable advantage of seeing the big picture.*

COMPREHENSIVE MARKETING PLAN

FOR

THE INTERNATIONAL WIDGET COMPANY
111 ANYSTREET
ANYTOWN, U.S.A. 11111

DATE
(last revision date)

THIS DOCUMENT IS CONFIDENTIAL
FOR AUTHORIZED PERSONNEL ONLY

Now we've got page one completed, we're on a roll! Let's keep going!

The Secret of Marketing

The secret of marketing is trying lots of different strategies by performing *modest* tests, keeping track of the results and, if the test is profitable, expanding the promotion to a larger audience. Unfortunately it's difficult for anyone to predict which strategy will outperform the others before you test.

Once the results of your baseline promotion are established, begin testing, *one at a time,* variations in the offering. The variations must be coded or identifiable at time of sale so that you can compare the results to the baseline. Once a variation shows a higher return that version will become your new baseline. Begin testing variations on the new baseline, *always* coding and tabulating results. Be aware that most of your promotions will not be profitable; that's why you must keep the test as small and inexpensive as possible (but large enough for you to obtain statistically meaningful results).

Part 1: your company

What makes your company, product or service better than the competition? In order to make your marketing plan sizzle, you must establish what makes your company stand out from the rest.

Define your company and its customers:

- Are you the newest in town?

- Are you the oldest and best-established in town?

- Are you the most experienced in the world?

- Do you sell low-cost products or services or do you sell the highest quality?

- Is your line the most advanced; is it the most time-proven?

_____

_____

_____

_____

_____

_____

_____

_____

_____

_____

_____

_____

_____

Part 2: goals

Define your short and long term goals for your company.

Where do you intend to be in the marketplace in:

1 year _____

5 years _____

10 years _____

Part 3: customers

Define your best customers:

• How did you get them?

• How can you duplicate that process to get new customers?

• Which media most cost effectively reaches that type of person?

_____

_____

_____

If you do not possess a good definition of your best customers above, how can you find them?

• Use personal interviews?

• Telephone each of them with a free offer and tell them you'd like to know more about them?

• Send each a questionnaire with a reward for answering?

Describe how you plan to find out more about your customers here.

_____

_____

_____

_____

_____

_____

Part 4: service

As Jay Abraham says, "You cannot provide too much service to your customers."

• What can you do to serve your customer better?

• Faster service?

• Informative newsletter?

• The most advanced techniques?

• Greet them by name?

• Ask each of them to offer you suggestions?

• Brainstorm with your distributors, suppliers, business associates?

• Ask your employees for their ideas.

• List your ideas for better service:

_____

_____

_____

_____

_____

_____

_____

_____

_____

_____

_____

You cannot provide too much service to your customers.

Part 5: USP (Unique Selling Proposition)

Describe why you are unique:

- List your companies or products and services features that makes you unique.

- What benefits do your customers think of when they hear your name?

_____

_____

_____

_____

What advantages do you offer your customers that no one else does?

_____

_____

_____

_____

Formulate a statement that describes your Unique Selling Proposition.

Your USP

Using the most important benefits, in the customer's eyes, formulate a statement that describes your USP (Unique Selling Proposition)

_e.g._

"I sell the highest quality fortune cookies in the world."

"Our diamonds have the lowest price markup in the industry"

"We know more about dry-cleaning than anyone west of the Pecos."

"We have the biggest selection of videotapes in Fairview."

"We're the only 24-hour, 7-day-a-week, pharmacy in the county."

"We have more plumbers than anyone so we can respond to your emergency in just one hour instead of one day."

Define your USP:

_____

_____

_____

If you came up empty on your USP, you will need to begin formulating one. Write some candidates below and if appropriate, call a meeting of some or all the people in your company to assist in establishing your USP. Ask your customers and your distributors for their suggestions on how you can serve them better. Discuss potential USPs with your suppliers; you may indeed discover that they can offer you a great deal of insight into what you need to do!

_____

_____

_____

_____

_____

_____

_____

_____

_____

_____

_____

_____

Part 6: Spreading the news!

Once you've established a USP, *tell your customers!!* Get the message to the news media. Paint the "motto" on your truck, print it on your business cards, and stationery, climb up on the roof and shout it through a megaphone, send your old and prospective new clients a letter and tell them how you can best solve their problems and meet their needs. You might use:

- press release to newspapers, radio, TV, magazines

- talk shows

- newsletter

- direct mail

- Yellow Pages

- billboards

- Internet, CompuServ, AOL (America OnLine), email

List your communications options here:

_____

_____

_____

_____

Your USP Action Plan

Establish schedule for the near-term implementation of "broadcasting" your USP.

_____

_____

_____

Part 7: Educate your customers!

Consumers, when considering buying a product or service often don't know much about the subject. Having unanswered questions leads to a hesitance in purchasing. You need to educate your prospective customers about the good and bad features. For example, if you researched 17 brands of suntan lotion to determine the one that caused the least skin irritation, best sunburn protection, and the most-natural–looking tan, tell the customers exactly what you did.

List below the information that your prospective buyers need.

_____

_____

_____

_____

_____

_____

_____

_____

_____

_____

_____

_____

_____

_____

_____

_____

Part 8: Prompt your customers!

- Tell Your Customers What to do

- Tell your customers exactly what action to take to benefit from your services

- Do you want them to come to the store by next Thursday to take advantage of this offer?

- Tell them where you are, provide a map or off ramps, directions, where to park.

- What hours are you open?

- Do you want him to phone you; of so what phone numbers including area code should they phone?

- Do they need to have a credit card ready? Which ones?

List the action(s) you want your customers to take:

_____

_____

_____

_____

_____

_____

_____

_____

_____

_____

_____

Tell your customers exactly what action to take to benefit from your services.

Part 9: Figuring the profits (or loss)

You must analyze each promotion to determine if it paid for itself and made a profit. You have a number of ways to gather the data necessary for your analysis:

- Design a worksheet on a pad of paper or in your computer.

- Direct your bookkeeper to keep track.

- Hire a firm that specializes in tracking data.

List your proposed methods of gathering this data:

_____

_____

_____

_____

_____

_____

_____

_____

_____

_____

_____

_____

_____

_____

_____

Part 10: Advertising do's and don'ts

Don't be funny or pompous.

Some businessmen have fallen into the trap of running "cute" or humorous advertising—stop it now!

Many fall into the trap of image building or self-aggrandizement; stop that too!

The only purpose of advertising is to make sales. Ads must make a total and convincing case for the customer to do business with you.

Every ad should demand a direct response. When preparing an ad keep your typical buyer in mind. In general, the longer the ad, the more information you will give and the better the response will be.

The more you tell, the more you sell.

Do not try to entertain or show off your literary skills, do not boast except about your super product or service.

What are your ads like now?

_____

_____

_____

_____

The more you tell, the more you sell!

Attention-grabbing headlines

When creating an ad, spend at least as much time on the headline of an ad as you do on the body. A change in headline can increase sales by a factor of five. Create a headline that specifically appeals to the prospective customers you can interest. In other words, if you're promoting something exclusively for vegetarians, try to screen out the meat eaters in the headline. The people you are trying to sell to must realize the ad contains something they may want. Just as in reading a newspaper people pick out which ad they wish to read by reading the headline. Practice some headlines.

Bonuses

Bonuses can give a big boost to your sales. What inexpensive but high perceived value bonuses can you include in your promotion? Candidate bonuses

_____

_____

_____

Guarantees

Your proposition needs to present a low risk to your customer.

Stress the guarantee and you've removed a roadblock to the sale.

- What can you guarantee or how can you guarantee longer or more widely?

- Can you offer a free trial?

- A free sample?

- Define a low-risk offer

_____

_____

_____

_____

_____

Be Specific

Never use generalities or platitudes when designing your promotion. They roll off your prospects like water off a bullfrog. To claim "We are the best," or "The quality of our eclairs is supreme," seldom achieves the desired result (i.e., sales). Be specific.

Here's some examples of specific offers, notice how these offers serve to 'screen out' non-prospects for purchase.

"Looking for a $1200 widescreen name brand television for just $798? We have 32 in stock."

"Health insurance for people over age 50 with *no physical, no waiting, no restrictions.*"

"Here are 18 quick-and-easy dinners for working women who are short of time for cooking."

"Used by long-distance runners from 27 different Olympic teams."

Reselling to your customers

Once you have a customer it's easier to re-sell him than find a new one. If you don't have products or services to follow up with, find a logical extension of what you do now. Resell to old customers over and over again. List how you plan to do this:

_____

_____

_____

_____

_____

_____

_____

_____

Part 11: Distribution

Your Market: Defining your markets and distribution channels

A major key to efficient and effective marketing is recognizing and segmenting your market. Look at your market in terms of clients and geography. How you distribute your product and the nature of the product itself will help you to define your market.

Are you focusing primarily on a local or limited area?

Are you a local retailer? Your geographical market would probably be a local or limited area (although you might employ the Internet to expand it...).

Do your distribution techniques include mail-order? Your geographical market would include a larger area.

Do you distribute through independent reps?

Is your product aimed at a regional or national market?

Does your product limit itself to a particular geographical area? (For instance, snow vehicles are best marketed in snow country)

Part 12: Your Instant Marketing Plan

Now that you've answered all those questions, it's time to generate your own *Instant Marketing Plan*. This doesn't mean that your plan won't change later; it's a plan that begins with the fundamentals, a plan you can implement today, then refine as your tests dictate.

1-The first step is free publicity. Usually this will start with press releases, although you can also initiate interviews with the media.

• Using your Unique Selling Proposition and your customer demographics, begin creating a press release. You may want to have a copywriter from your local newspaper assist you, or you can contact a professional who specializes in press releases. For such professional assistance, you should check your Yellow Pages under "Advertising" or "Public Relations Agencies."

- Your next step is to choose who should receive your press releases. As appropriate, this can be your local town or city, county, state (or province), nation or worldwide. You may obtain lists from your local Chamber of Commerce, county or state (province) business development agencies, or even a media distribution service such as MDS Media Distribution Services PRA Group. You can reach them at (800) 637-3282.

Request their brochures and order their booklet. You'll be amazed at the wealth of information you'll get. Also call Para Publishing's fax-on-demand from your fax machine and print out Para's list categories. Dial 805 968-8947 and follow the easy voice prompts.

2-All future (paid) advertising should be designated to promote a direct response. Much advertising today is primarily image-building and doesn't prompt the reader or listener to take action. From now on your ads will be designed to provoke a response. Your ads should give reasons why your merchandise or service is the best, the least expensive or the most reliable. It should promise results and back that promise with a warranty. It should invite the reader or listener to come to your place of business, send in money or dial your number. A direct-mail campaign should be high on your list or priorities. Again, this can be on a local level (all of the Norwegians or dentists or fly fishermen or Corvette owners in your town), or as appropriate on a county, state (province), national or worldwide level. List sources can be expanded to include such entities as clubs, state (or province) department of motor vehicles, to national list brokers. Again, look in the *Yellow Pages.*

3-Test everything. Code all of your promotions and keep records of responses. When one works, use it as your basic campaign and run variations whereby you change only one variable at a time. Change the headline, or the price, or throw in a free gift, *etc.,* and keep records of the subsequent results. When you identify a variation that works best among the variables you've chosen to test, you establish that element as a new "temporarily-fixed" item and you can proceed with changes to the other variables.

4-Once you've gained a new customer, try for repeat business. It's much easier to keep a customer than replace him. Look for other products and services that will keep him (or her) coming back. For example, a dry cleaner could publish a simple newsletter that describes procedures for preventing moth damage, or how to pack for a trip. Are such extra efforts likely to pay off for you? You bet!

In the following chapters you'll discover how to refine these concepts and explore others. But what you've learned in this chapter should form the foundation for your marketing plan.

Chapter 3

Refining Your Marketing Plan

What form should your marketing plan take? Well, it's up to you, but I suggest a relaxed, easy-to-read format. It's also a good idea to have your plan bound in a way that's easy to take apart and update, especially in the beginning when you begin adding, modifying and refining it. A three-ring binder works well.

You've already seen an example of a title page. For the plan itself, you may wish to loosely follow the questions that guided you through the information needed for a basic marketing plan. Now the actual text of your document may read something like this:

PART I: OUR ORGANIZATION

A. The International Widget Company: a quick history.

In order to know where our company is headed, we need to know where it's been. To understand our company, current and future sales people, advertising people and public relations employees need to understand our history, and make current and future decisions with the successes and failures of the past in mind. Let's start at the beginning:

"The International Widget Company was founded in 1978. Our founder, seeing a public need for a Jim-Jam that would could be afforded by the less-affluent consumer, improved and streamlined a

manufacturing process to provide a quality Jim-Jam at a reduced price. The new, less-expensive Jim-Jam was well received by the target market. The International Widget Company became known for its low price and quality. Capitalizing on that reputation, Widget Company has developed a complete line of related, low-priced, quality products that continues the success of the Jim-Jam.

Beginning with just four employees in a one-room rented building, the Widget Company expanded within one year to twelve employees with a total annual payroll of nearly one million dollars. Sales figures for the first year were such-and-such, increasing to such-and-such in just three years..." and so on. Be sure to include all the major financial gains or serious set backs the company has experienced. Be thorough. Include any newspaper articles or trade magazine articles written about your company in the appendix, and record any effects (in both short-term and long-term aspects) those articles had on your business. In short, tell a complete story about the company, starting at the beginning and ending at the end.

Use a comfortable style

As you can see, writing all parts of your marketing plan text is merely a matter of gathering your answers to your questions into readable statements. Use the approach that is most comfortable for you. It's quite okay to use a conversational style in the document. You may wish to merely list some of the information. If you or your marketing team are visually oriented, use diagrams or drawings to present or clarify some of the material. Relax! If you find it daunting or difficult to write, just write it out as if you were telling a friend all about your company. Then let the plan sit for a couple of days and go back to it. You may find much of it is just fine and some of it needs to be restated or reorganized. If you expect perfection on the first try you will intimidate yourself and make the writing process much more difficult. In the words of E.B. White, *"Remember, it is no sign of weakness or defeat that your manuscript ends up in need of major surgery. This is a common occurrence in all writing, and among the best writers."* Very likely, you will be a bit vague on some of the information. That is to be expected. This basic plan is really more of a first draft—you will want to make changes before you formally adopt it as your official marketing plan. Reading the material in the remainder of this book will help you refine your plan and will suggest some ideas you may want to include.

After typing your plan up, the logical next step is presenting it to your marketing managers (or whoever you've designated for such a role) as a first draft and asking for their input.

Refining your plan

It's time to take that basic plan and polish it up a bit. Let's do it!

Refining your plan should be an ongoing process for the life of your company. In the beginning, it will probably require a bit of work and time. This is to be expected because, as I said, it is really a first draft. Sharing this first draft with your marketing managers and getting their input is an important step, but first let's do a little fine tuning. The time you spend on refining the plan is time spent learning the facts about your company, your market, and your marketing strategy. This is invaluable information to you and your marketing team. Knowing your marketing goals and focusing on them is, after all, the purpose of a formal written program.

Refining your plan should be an ongoing process for the life of your company.

So, even while you work on your plan, it is fulfilling its purpose!

Ready to do some polishing? To make it easy, let's go at it section-by-section in the same order that the questions were laid out.

Your organization history

While a sense of your company's history is important for perspective, it's important to your marketing plan in another way, as well. As the old question goes, "How can you know where you're going, if you don't know where you've been?" In addition, your company's history determines your methods for getting there; your plan is dependent upon where you are in your own history.

If your organization is quite new, you will of necessity need to focus more heavily on the development of strategy. New companies without a marketing history are forced to depend on researching the experiences of other companies (or suffer more of their own costly mistakes). In addition, they will have to focus on testing distribution and promotional strategies. They will be building a bridge.

Older companies have a history to refer to and know which strategies work and which don't. Although they must be aware of changes occurring in the marketplace that may change the effectiveness of proven strategies, they may focus on fine-tuning established strategies for growth and implementing those changes that they deem necessary to accomplish their objectives. These companies will be maintaining and strengthening their bridge.

Part II—YOUR MARKET AND YOUR COMPETITION

Market overview

Nearly all markets are undergoing major changes. Technology, changing customer needs, government regulation, more and tougher competition—all this and more—are affecting the overall marketplace. In light of the rapid changes in today's market, it is extremely important to have a clear and accurate view of your market to assess your market position and strategy. You need to know what others are trying, and have tried, to avoid approaches that don't work.

In the overall market for your product, identifying trends that will affect your marketing strategy is important. Logically, the first trend to pin down is the growth trend. Is your market demand growing or shrinking?

Of course, a growing demand sounds like an ideal market situation. But growing demand does not necessarily mean unlimited opportunity. Consider these questions: Has competition been stepped up because of the growth trend? Is every company on your block jumping in to take advantage of the growing demand? Opportunity may still be knocking, but if you must compete with significant competition, you must have a marketing strategy to meet the challenge.

A shrinking market, on the face of it, does not sound promising. However, a close look may reveal opportunity. Has the competition also shrunk? Have others bailed out because the market is shrinking? This may open opportunity for the brave few who

Is your market demand growing or shrinking?

remain. But those few must develop a strategy that deals efficiently with the situation.

Some key trends are not quite so easily pinned down. Social, cultural, and political trends, if correctly interpreted, can be tremendously valuable in developing new products or successful new strategies for marketing old products. As times change, the needs of your customers change and your product benefit emphasis may require adjustment.

Separating real trends from fads isn't always easy.

For instance, look at the emphasis on "low fat" in the food industry today. Some of these low fat foods have always been low in fat, but it was not a benefit that was emphasized until relatively recently because it was not perceived as a benefit. Then along came a general health food trend, and everyone who was marketing a naturally lowfat product suddenly began shouting it from the rooftops. Others rushed to develop lowfat versions of favorite foods so they, too, could shout from the rooftops.

Spotting the market trends and separating real trends from fads isn't always easy, and capitalizing on them can be tricky. But it's essential to marketing. Remember, the market demand controls you; you cannot control the market.

It may seem that a new and innovative product creates its own market. But on closer examination, you will find that the basic need it satisfies was there before the product came along. The demand was created not by the product; it was created by social, political, or cultural trends. A new product (or an existing one, for that matter) must provide a benefit that is already in demand. The trick is to emphasize the benefits that satisfy that demand.

Looking at the "whys" of market trends may reveal important information. Should a new marketing angle be adopted? Sometimes a seemingly small shift in emphasis is effective. Sometimes a completely new strategy is called for.

Segmenting your markets

Now I'm going to tell you that what we've been discussing doesn't exist! There is no such thing as "the market"—there are only market segments. Identifying the segments that are relevant to your marketing plan is extremely important. Segmenting your markets as narrowly as possible in terms of geography, clients, and niches is a key to efficient marketing.

Geographical segmentation may depend upon the nature of your product, or it may depend upon your distribution method. If the need for your product is by nature confined to a particular geographical region, identify that area. If your distribution method is limited to a particular area, target your distribution territory precisely. Focus your marketing efforts on your targeted area. National advertising, for instance, is of little worth for a regional product or service.

Clientele segmentation is defining your market in terms of who will be interested in your product. Obviously the market for women's cosmetics would naturally fall into segmenting by gender, although husbands, fathers, brothers, sons and boyfriends are significant (gift) purchasers of certain women's products. But certain cosmetic products may lead to segmenting by age or race as well. Narrow it down as closely as possible and focus your marketing energy (and dollars) on the narrow segment that you target.

Focus your marketing efforts on your targeted area.

Niche markets are very narrow market segments (just *slices,* really). Niche markets, because of their size, may limit growth but can be lucrative if limited competition allows for higher prices. It's important when catering to a niche market to hold down marketing expenditures. You must employ a highly-focused marketing strategy, since the dollar value of a niche market is by definition smaller than that of the larger markets.

You may find that your product line requires individual segmentation for individual products. In this case, each product needs its own marketing strategy and should have its own marketing plan spelled out within your company marketing plan.

A demographic and psychographic view of your market

Defining your primary customer is important; successful marketing involves discovering who makes the purchasing decisions and what influences those decisions. You're probably quite familiar with your best customers. If you're not, you should be. Recapping your experiences with those customers and using your firsthand knowledge and opinions are OK to begin with, but a sound marketing plan should not be built on off-the-cuff guesses. Many of your guesses are perhaps very accurate but they must backed by research and informed, thoughtful consideration. Here's where the real polishing begins. Let's get down to some in-depth analysis. As you progress with refining your plan, it is important to gather knowledge about your clients. Research materials you may want to use include: your own observations and customer surveys; libraries; newspaper business pages; business and industry journals; banks; national, state, and local government departments, civic organizations, *Yellow Pages,* and Small Business Association resources.

Dealing face-to-face with your clients will lend itself to some relatively easy independent research. Many things can be ascertained without directly asking questions. Gender will be obvious. Age may be a bit trickier, but within general categories (such as over 40 and under 40), your approximations should work reasonably well for you. You may also be able to determine fairly accurately their education level, income class, and marital status. What area they live in may be obtained by asking them in general conversation or from their bank checks. Where they live is helpful to your marketing strategy in itself as well as an indicator of income level. Use charts to help you tabulate the information.

If you do not deal face-to-face with your clients or are uncomfortable with observing and charting facts about them, try customer response surveys. A telephone survey was successful for me. I collected clients' telephone numbers for several months. Then I phoned them to tell them that I was sending them a free gift (a pamphlet updating information I had sold them previously). Just from speaking with them, I could determine gender, but I felt a bit nervous about asking their ages at first. My anxiety proved to be groundless, however. After informing them that they would be receiving a free gift, I just plunged in with, *"We're attempting to learn a little more about our customers. Would you mind telling me whether you are over or under 40 years old?"* Without exception they answered without taking offense!

Another method of compiling client information is using a written survey. This works well if you have neither visual contact nor telephone numbers. Use a printed questionnaire (make it short and easy with boxes to check) that you either hand to your client or enclose with your product. Just make certain that your question-naire is intelligently and efficiently laid out, and test it on a few friends first before you finalize the design. Offer a free gift for responding or enter the response in a contest.

Bear in mind that the actual purchaser may not be the decision maker. Whether you are involved in business-to-business marketing or in consumer marketing, purchase decisions may not be made by the person doing the purchasing.

Make use of research done by others. Search for articles and information about your industry in newspaper business pages, industry journals, libraries, and computerized databases. Your library may conduct the search for a nominal charge. Try one of the online services such as *CompuServe* or *America Online*, or hire a consultant who specializes in database searches. The Small Business Association, the Department of Commerce, the Bureau of Labor Statistics, the Census Bureau, your local Chamber of Commerce, state and local governmental departments, and civic organizations are good sources to approach for industry research.

Once you have pinned down your primary customer demographically (in terms such as age, income level, sex, geographic location, and education level), you will have a merchandising target. This will help you to construct your merchandising attempts properly. But what will you appeal to? What influences their purchasing decisions? What are their needs? What benefits should you emphasize?

To answer these questions, you need a psychographic profile of your

Make certain that your questionnaire is intelligently laid out.

target market. Don't be alarmed if you have two demographic models that seem to be fairly equally represented. Merely develop a psychographic profile for each. A psychographic profile will tell you what needs your product is satisfying for your customers. These are the benefits that a successful marketing campaign will emphasize. If you want to persuade people to buy your product, you must know what human advantages your customer will gain. You must ferret out every possible inducement and weigh each one in relation to your target customer.

First we will take a look at the "average" person. These views will necessarily be simplified and incomplete. There really is no such thing as an average person and, anyway, your customer is special, not average. However, some basic human needs are common to a majority of people, so our average person may reveal some important characteristics for you to consider.

The "average" person wants to increase:

- financial, physical, mental well being

- emotional, social, and spiritual well-being

- satisfaction, self-respect, and security

He seeks to lessen, eliminate, or avoid:

- doubts, risks, and mistakes

- worries, losses, and embarrassments

- boredom

He seeks to decrease fear of:

- Poverty or discomfort

- Illness or accident

He seeks to decrease fear of loss of:

- business
- personal or social prestige
- advancement

The average person wants:

- more money
- success
- more comfort
- better health
- more leisure and enjoyment
- improved appearance
- acceptance and praise
- greater popularity and social advancement
- security—now and in old age

What does this all really mean? For instance, most people want more money. Why? They don't want to worry about where their next dollar is coming from. They want money for savings, spending, or perhaps giving to others. But it isn't just the money that's important here. It's what the money can do for them. They want security and promise of a fulfilling retirement that savings can give them. They want the improved quality of life. They want to know they have capability and more money will give them pride of accomplishment. More money will allow them to buy the clothes, car, and new home they want for improved physical appearance and social acceptance. People feel good about themselves when they feel attractive and successful.

You see? The idea is to examine below the surface. If people want more money and you aren't in the business of giving them more money, look into the "whys." Of course, you can offer to save them money by offering a bargain price—in a way that's giving them more money. But if you look deeper, perhaps you can offer them an improved physical appearance or improve their feeling of accomplishment.

Let's look into the other categories listed:

They want success for the pride of accomplishment to be gained from it through doing things well and overcoming competition and other obstacles. More comfort will bring them ease, convenience, and self-indulgences. An enhancement of strength and vigor comes with good health. With more leisure will be opportunities to travel, play, rest, have hobbies, and seek self improvement. They want enjoyment from food, entertainment, drink, and other pleasant physical contacts. A wish for an improved appearance is a desire for a better physical build, beauty, style, and cleanliness. Acceptance and praise is an appreciation of appearance, knowledge, judgement, or superiority. Greater popularity and social advancement is acceptance and praise.

What else do we know about "the average person"? Well, how about some things he (or she) may want in a product.

In a product, the average person may want:
- better quality

- a lower price

- time-saving features

- convenience

- state-of-the-art design

- prestige

- ease of use

- multiple capabilities

- durability

- solutions

- effectiveness

- to make money

- to save money

- benefits

Keep in mind that the average person may not want what you think he wants. He or she will buy your product to satisfy an emotional need as well as a rational need. His emotions and his perception of himself and your product will influence his purchasing decisions. This may be done consciously, unconsciously, or both. What we are talking about here is, of course, benefits. Every marketing proposition has basic differences, but ultimately every marketing proposition hinges on benefits. Whatever you may be selling, you are marketing benefits. Marketing is about emotional and financial issues—emotional things such as love, fear, hope, greed and guilt, and financial things such as profits and value.

The marketer needs to know his product, inside and out. Knowing it in a pictorial or physical way is just the beginning. You must experience its values and benefits and see how a customer will perceive its benefits. With this fundamental involvement, you can create the good, effective, and powerful marketing that emphasizes the advantages, appeals and benefits your customer will benefit from by having chosen your product. Concentrate on what your product will do for your customer.

But what exactly does your customer want? Your customer is a special person, not the "average person" we've been discussing. Determining what your targeted "special" person is like involves dealing with both the conscious and the unconscious level.

On the conscious or reasoning level, your customer may choose a product for such reasons as:

- **Value**—The customer is most concerned with value... *i.e.*, a good deal. Whatever he buys, he (or she) wants it to be worth the price.

- **Durability**—The customer who is more concerned with reliability than cost. The product he buys must work well; it must be without defects.

- **Innovation**—The customer is looking for the new and innovative. He wants a product that is exciting, revolutionary, state-of-the-art.

Looking at your target customers' professions can reveal a clues for determining what type of buyers they are. Value-seeking buyers are often employed in professions that are: traditional (law enforcement, for example), highly budget–oriented (entrepreneurs and accountants, for example), or lower income. Those buyers seeking durability in their purchasing choices often work in professions that tend to be middle-class conservative such as bankers, brokers, career military, middle-to-senior management, and the medical and educational fields. The innovation buyers include people in higher income and less-structured fields such as performing arts, fine arts, athletics, inventors, senior executives, and politicians.

> **Concentrate on what your product will do for your customer.**

On the unconscious or emotional level, your customer may choose a product because he/she is:

- **Idea oriented**— Getting his main gratification from interacting with his own ideas, he's concerned with control without being involved, having it his own way, creating his own thing, controlling his own world;

- **Object oriented**—Getting his main gratification from interacting with inanimate objects or data, he likes reliability, no risks, zero defects, guarantees, statistics, proven systems and technology—something he can confidently rely upon;

- **People oriented**—Getting his main gratification from interacting with people, he likes to feel special or make someone else feel special, he wants to be a hit with his team.

To determine the orientation of your primary customer base, look at their professions again. Although a person may be employed in a job he just doesn't like, the orientation of his work can still be an indicator of what his personal orientation is. For example, a newspaper reporter may loathe his job of covering city council meetings and writing articles about crime and sewer projects. Still, his orientation as a person who loves the written word and current events may hold true—it's just that our reporter would rather be a novelist than a reporter; an auto mechanic may dislike the daily drudgery of tuning carburetors or bleeding brake lines, but he may love cars and have dreams of being a Formula One driver.

So pay attention to the professional orientation of your targeted customer. What work he is doing will tell you something about the person. Just what does his job require him to think about and interact with every day? Does he work with ideas, people or objects? Does he sit down, use his mind, or walk around a lot and rely on his body to provide labor? Maybe he works seated, but perform mindless tasks, such as assembling or inspecting. Think about it.

At this point in your marketing plan your objective is to define the geographic and socioeconomic parameters of your market. This definition will be pivotal in designing your positioning strategy and your Unique Selling Proposition (in Part Three of your plan).

Current marketing activities

This section surveys the marketing efforts you are currently engaged in, or which you perform during scheduled times throughout the year. Be sure to complete the discussion with your reasons for choosing the particular activities and media that you use.

Defining your competition

Now the BIG rule for this section is: Don't minimize your competition! Be honest with yourself. If the others are doing a better job than you in your market area, then admit it. Don't poke your head in the sand! Just be prepared to overhaul your marketing plan to do something about it!

In today's market, success is dependent upon knowing what your competition is doing, then planning and implementing a strategy to deal with them. Marketing strategists who don't take into account the increasingly aggressive tactics of the competition are not protecting their share of the market. They're not losing their market share, they're giving it away!

The first step is identifying your competition. This may seem simple enough at first glance, but it isn't as obvious as you may think. If you listed your competitors quickly and with little thought, you've probably made an incomplete list. For instance, you've no doubt

In today's market, success is dependent upon knowing what your competition is doing.

listed other businesses of a similar size and mission—if you have a hardware store or a restaurant, you probably listed the other hardware stores and restaurants in your marketing area.

This is a good beginning, but let's look a little deeper. Are there other competitors out there that you're ignoring? If you have a hardware store, have you listed the discount chain stores and the building supply companies? Sometimes the less-obvious competition consists of the very companies that are making the greatest inroads into your market.

You've looked at the competition in your area, but have you considered the distant companies using different distribution channels? Are you competing with mail-order companies? Check it out. Today's mail-order companies deal in a wide variety of products that seemed improbable for then to offer just yesterday—and many of them are doing it quite successfully! Identify your direct competitors, those who are targeting at least some of your segment and positioning themselves similarly. Your marketing strategy will have to meet them head-on. Also identify *potential* competitors who may be targeting a small portion of your market or have the capacity to do so. Part of your marketing strategy should be to keep a close eye on these companies. They might blossom overnight into full blown competition.

Have a contingency plan! Be ready to accept the competitive challenge as soon as one of them makes a move into your market segments. Keep a broad view. Identifying your competition, watching it closely, and predicting the new sources such competition may come from, will help protect you from being caught

Identify potential competitors who may be targeting a small portion of your market.

unprepared. Stay up-to-date. Social, cultural, and political trends may be harbingers of new competition. For instance, how will the increasing technology of personal computing affect your business? Will new competition such as computer marketing bear watching?

After identifying your competition, analyze their tactics. Know how your product stacks up in comparison to their product. Know what benefits they do and don't emphasize. If your products are similar and your competition is not stressing benefits that you feel are selling points, hit those benefits hard in your marketing. How can you add benefits that the competition is not providing, such as better service or free delivery? Know (or develop) your strong points in comparison to your competition and focus on them.

Market projections, risks, resources

Spend some time on this section. It's extremely important. Marketing can be compared to football—you must grab the opportunities and run for the goalposts before the competition has a chance to respond and knock you out of the play. But you must have a gameplan that prepares you to assess the risks and the options involved. If the team isn't ready for a particular play and you push it, you could get badly hurt.

Be sure to spend some time determining your resources. You need to know exactly what your resources are and how they can be most effectively used. If you are aware of what your people are capable of, what sources of capital you have, and how time can be best employed, you'll be more prepared to effectively tackle the opportunities that come along.

After identifying your competition, analyze their tactics.

PART III—YOUR MARKETING STRATEGY

Your marketing strategy goals

Without clear goals, it's difficult to develop an effective marketing strategy and measure your progress. Without realistic, challenging objectives, your incentive will be diminished. Setting goals with time periods clearly spelled-out gives you a measuring stick. When you know where you want to be and when you want to be there, a glimpse at your current situation should tell you whether your progress is satisfactory.

Your stated goals should not be limited to volume or profits (though they should definitely be included). Set goals for such things as customer satisfaction, repeat business, territory expansion, and employee training as well.

How you are perceived by your customers

How your customers perceive you will have an effect on how you should market your product. For instance, if your customers are sold on a widget but need to decide what brand they should buy, it would be unnecessary to attempt to convince them they want a widget. You will want to tell them why they should buy your widget. You won't be out there extolling the virtues of a product; you'll be out there extolling the virtues of your product brand (or, perhaps, your trademarked service: "We Conduit Electrical", or "10S NE1" Tennis Pros). How you are perceived in relation to your competition also gives you an indication of the slant you should use in marketing your product. Is your product offered at a premium price? Then emphasize the benefits of selecting your high-quality

Setting goals with time periods spelled-out gives you a measuring stick.

product. Give your customer solid reasons for paying more.

How you wish to be perceived

This is a matter of determining the benefits of your product that the customers should be aware of. What would you like for their immediate (conscious or subconscious) response to your product name to be? You'd probably be pleased with *"Oh, an International Widget? The best quality on the market,"* or *"A real value."*

Your USP and your positioning strategy

Your Unique Selling Proposition (or USP) is different from your Positioning Statement. Your USP is a statement of the unique qualities and benefits that a customer sees in doing business with you and no one else; it's the emotionally-compelling message that conveys to your customer what you're really selling (benefits). Your USP is stated in terms of benefits to your clients.

Your Positioning Statement is a declaration (more literal and less emotional than USP) of how your company "fits" in the marketplace. It is a definition of who you are. Both are vital to your marketing strategy. Both should be kept to the forefront and emphasized in everything you do. All of your marketing personnel need to be aware of these statements—they are a definition of who and what you are. Positioning sets you apart from the competition and makes you more desirable in the customers eye. It takes into account the psychographics of your customer, how he perceives what you sell and how he perceives your enterprise in relation to your competition.

One way to determine what positioning stance to consider is to write down the benefits your rivals are stressing. Include all your direct competition. From this you can make positioning decisions. If, for example, everyone else is emphasizing high quality, you can fight it out with all of them, or you can look for the weak spots and stress them. If few are mentioning service, you may find it more beneficial to strongly emphasize your quality service in combination with your high quality product. Your positioning should be based upon your knowledge of your product, your customer profile, and your competitions' positioning.

With your Unique Selling Proposition and your Positioning Statement firmly in mind, you can keep your marketing strategy consistent. Without them clearly in mind, you may end up sending mixed signals that will confuse your customers. They'll get the impression that you don't know who you are and what your product or service is. Successful marketing projects a confidence about what your company is doing.

Successful marketing projects a confidence about what your company is doing.

Your sales plan

Your sales plan should include size of sales team, training programs and schedules, management training and schedules, and dealer programs. Also include a discussion of future changes and improvements. Include such things as increasing your sales force or dealer sites, what additional resources you will need and the timeframe for making the changes.

Your sales-promotion plan

Detail your existing and planned sales promotions. Include themes and budgets.

PART IV: YOUR COMMUNICATIONS STRATEGY

Advertising campaigns

Your advertising objective is to get the right message to the right people in a cost-effective and timely manner. What is the right message?

Much, of course depends upon your product, your USP, your positioning. But some general concepts are quite applicable to almost any advertising campaign. Educate your customer. You will gain your customers' trust if you objectively educate them about all of the products of interest to them. They want to understand about your product(s).

Tell your clients what unique advantages you offer them. Determine which needs you can fulfill for your customers. Then talk to your clients and prospects and let them tell you which needs they most want filled. Then fill those needs that you can. But **tell them.** Tactfully point out that you listened and you are doing something about it. Do you have a superior service program or guarantee? **Tell them!** Are you the only supplier in town who offers free installation or free service for the first twelve months? **Tell them!** Do you choose "only the best" products to offer your customers? **Tell them!** People won't know these wonderful things about you or your product unless you point it out.

Tell your customers why. If your product or service is being offered at a premium price, tell them why? Is it because it is of premium quality? What makes it premium quality? Finer materials? More durable? On the other hand, why are you offering at an especially

> *Your advertising objective is to get the right message to the right people in a cost-effective and timely manner.*

low price? Do you need to bail out because the season is coming to an end? Is it an introductory offer to a new customer? Do you operate with lower overhead than your competition? Tell them why they should choose to do business with you.

Focus on your customer. Make each ad a compelling salesman for your merchandise. It should be educational, informative, complete and compelling. Answer all the immediate questions and inform the customer of the benefits that you can deliver. Promise performance or results.

Advertising is selling

Tell your customer what he needs to do. After you give him a brief education, tell him/her explicitly what to do now to obtain your product or service. Know how much of your budget will be spent on each campaign, on each medium. Spell it out. Devise testing for every element of your advertising. Test different headlines, copy, themes, media, to develop maximum performance from all advertising you do. Test pricing and packaging, different salesman, different emphases, test everything. When you find a successful combination, work it. Don't pull it while it's working. You will get tired of the successful ad before your customers do. As long as it's working, use it. But keep assessing its effectiveness. Devise a method to keep record of the effectiveness of every campaign.

Devise testing for every element of your advertising.

Chapter 4

Effective Marketing

Now, some straightforward talk for you: Every company is marketing-intensive. Every company is in the business of generating and retaining customers. Every company needs effective marketing. Some folks just don't realize it.

Marketing must lead the company. Marketing must focus upon customer satisfaction, and that must be your overriding objective for your company. That's what brings your customers back again and again.

Everything, everything depends upon recognizing and satisfying your customers needs. From generating new customers to reselling current and past customers, it all hinges on benefits—the satisfaction of your customers' needs.

Unique Selling Proposition

For effective marketing, it is imperative that you clearly define your Unique Selling Proposition (or USP). You say, *"Buy from us."* The customer says, *"Why?"* Your answer is a clue to the USP you are now operating with—even though you have never really developed one formally.

Your USP is the statement of the distinguishing advantage you should trumpet in *all* of your marketing, advertising, and sales

> **Marketing must be your overriding objective for your company.**

efforts. Every sales effort you put before your customers should focus on your USP. I'm talking about in-store sales efforts as well as advertising.

Benefits. Your *Unique Selling Proposition* (USP) is stated in the form of benefits to your clients—the unique qualities and benefits that a customer sees in you but in no one else. It uses the emotionally-compelling words that convey to your customer that what you're really selling is BENEFITS. Remember that your customers are purchasing satisfaction of their needs. Okay, you no doubt know what the features of your product or service are. All you need to do is translate those features into benefits.

Take a blank sheet of paper. Draw a line down the center. Headline one side "FEATURES." Headline the other side "BENEFITS." Now on the "FEATURES" side list every feature of your product that you can think of. Once you have all the features listed, take them one at a time and translate them into benefits. Look at it from your customers' point of view. Take each feature and ask yourself, "What good will this feature do me?" Write your answers in plain everyday terms. But be specific.

For instance, if you happen to be selling a book about memory improvement, what is the feature? It improves your memory. What good will this do your customer; in other words, what are its *benefits*? *"You'll be able to perform amazing feats of memory." "You'll astound your friends, impress your boss." "You'll never be embarrassed again by forgetting someone's name." "You'll never forget your anniversary." "Never forget an important birthday." "You'll feel smarter, more confident."*

Remember that your customers are purchasing satisfaction of their needs.

Do you think your customers want your goods for sound practical reasons? They may not want what you think they want. They are choosing your product (or service) to gratify an emotional need or desire. What you are selling is benefits, a symbol of that gratification.

Consider this: If there's a dozen companies selling essentially the same gadget that you are selling, why do your customers choose to buy yours? Is it because they perceive yours to be a better value? Better quality? Defect free? More exciting? More powerful? How will purchasing from you make them feel better? If you have a truly outstanding gadget that differs radically (and favorably) from all the others on the market, you have an obvious selling point. But only if prospective customers perceive the difference and see it as favorable. And only if the perceived difference will gratify an existing emotional need.

Perhaps there is no basic difference between your gadget and the thirteen others on the market. Does it matter? *Not really*. The perceived difference is what matters—the perceived benefits of choosing your product. Everyone's reality is, after all, perception. What your customer perceives to be true about your product or service is true. Your USP, then, focuses on the customer's perception of your product in terms of gratifying emotional needs and desires. It emphasizes the favorable perceived benefits or strives to change unfavorable current perceptions.

How do we determine what the customer wants?

How do we determine what the customer wants and, therefore, what our USP focus should be?

What your customer perceives to be true about your product or service is true.

You must address your customers' needs—needs they have been developing all of their lives. You cannot develop those needs; you must respond to them. Your USP is a response to your customers as people, human beings with needs and desires already developed. Your Unique Selling Proposition depends entirely on the specific market niche you are targeting. The focus of every successful business is the customer and the customer's needs and wants.

Knowing your customer demographically and psychographically, knowing your targeted niche, is a good beginning. It is a place to start, but "we don't have the right or the power to predetermine what the marketplace wants." We can't tell people what they want; we must provide them what they want. This is determined by testing one approach against another. **Testing—price, focus, offer, package, headline, bonus, every variable—is the best way for you to find out what the marketplace wants.**

Positioning Statement

The results of the testing will also be helpful in determining your positioning. Positioning sets you apart from the competition. It's a more literal and less emotional statement than your USP is. Your Positioning Statement is a declaration of where your company "fits" in the marketplace. It takes into account how your customers perceive what you sell and how they see you in relation to your competition.

Testing is the best way for you to find out what the marketplace wants.

Using Your USP and Positioning Statement

"Appeal to the reason, by all means. Give people a logical excuse for buying, one that they can tell to their friends and use to salve their own consciences. But if you want to sell goods, if you want action of any kind, base your real urge upon some primary emotion!"—Robert Collier

Do you recognize them? The first paragraph covers Positioning; the second covers USP. You will find one approach—one combination—that outpulls all of the others as a result of your testing. Develop your USP and positioning around this winning combination. Then use them. They are *vital* to your creating a strong, consistent marketing strategy. They should be reflected in your packaging and product design, your advertising and company slogans, your training of personnel, and in every sales effort.

You (and any business) have only three resources—talent, capital, and time. For effective marketing, all of these resources must be focused on the same priorities. The point of a marketing plan is to achieve this focus—moving everyone in the same direction. Your USP and positioning are your focusing points.

Testing

Successful marketing is dynamic. To remain dynamic, the formulation of your USP and positioning should not signal an end to testing. It is, rather, a beginning. Keep experimenting, keep testing to unocver even more effective approaches. Test different:

- headlines
- body copy

> **Keep experimenting, keep testing to uncover even more effective approaches.**

- themes

- emphases

- prices

- packages

- offers

- approaches

Test everything— even the "little" things.

Test everything—even the "little" things. Point of fact, there is no "little" thing in marketing. Everything counts. Sometimes it's the radio (or the cup holder) that sells the car. *Always* test. Strange and weird things can happen if you don't. An insurance company sent out 50,000 untested letters "selling" an umbrella type of coverage. They got back 275 responses—most ordering a real (raindrop-repelling–style) umbrella!

When one approach starts working, you begin testing other approaches. This is important, because every approach has a life cycle. Sooner or later it will run out of gas. Continuous testing will ensure that you have another approach to fall back on when that happens. But don't abandon an approach that is working well just because you are tired of it. Chances are you will become tired of a campaign before your customers do.

Educate Your Customers

Finding out what your customer wants through testing (or simply by asking), and responding with unique advantages won't be appreciated—unless your customer knows about it. Tell them. Educate them. It's your responsibility to communicate to them what you've done for them. If your gadget or your service offers features the others don't, make certain your customers are made aware of the attendant *benefits*. If your gadget is made of higher-quality materials or is handmade for greater dependability, let them know. If your offer includes warranties and extended service, point it out.

Advantages can be appreciated (and thus acted upon) only if prospective customers perceive the difference, and only if the perceived difference will gratify an existing emotional need. Advertising in print or over the airwaves is exactly the same as salesmanship in person. It is your leverage—a multiplication of your sales efforts. It should, then, be a complete case for your product.

Every ad should be educational and informative. Each should point out what you have done for your customer and include all of the unique advantages. Your prospects want to know—*must* know— about your merchandise or services so they can make an intelligent purchasing decision. Give them the education—briefly—that they want. Give them the factual, specific reasons why your product is superior to the others. Communicate to them how your product will improve their lives or situations or save them time and money.

The customers don't much care about your business—how long you've been in business, how big it is, *etc*. What they care about is what benefits they will realize if they buy from you. They want to know about the product, service, quality, guarantees. How will they benefit by purchasing from you rather than your competitors? You must give them a reason to buy from you, not just tell them how wonderful you are.

Answer all of the major questions you anticipate your customers would ask if you were selling in person. If you are offering your

> **You must give them a reason to buy from you, not just tell them how wonderful you are.**

product at an exceptionally low price; tell your customers *why* it's such an exciting low price. Why? They won't appreciate what you're doing unless they know. And they won't know it's an exceptional value unless you educate them. Then give them the reasons why you're doing it. Give them the truth. Are you overstocked? Is the stock locking up your cash flow? Tell them: "We goofed. We are overstocked on gadget's and it's tying up cash we need for operating expenses." Then make the offer exclusive with:

- *"But we're making this offer only to valued customers like you."*

-or-

- *"But we're making this offer only to people who buy our widget."*

-or-

- *"But we're making this offer only to first-time customers like you."*

You get the picture. The value perception on your offer increases if its perceived as not available to everyone.

Take Away the Risk

Most customers see themselves as taking all the risk. Turn it around. Take the risk upon yourself. Emphasize the money-back guarantee or risk-free warranty.

If you can, include a bonus item that the customer can keep even if returning the product under the money-back guarantee. In the customers' eyes this puts the risk squarely on you.

Tell Them What To Do

Then tell them explicitly what to do to purchase your product or try your service. Be specific. Tell them how and where they can obtain your product. Instruct them how to respond: *"pick up your phone now," "go to your local Toy Shoppe today."* Be specific: *"dial 1•888•888•8888 and ask for Gadgie-toy by name."*

Bonus items

Bonus items or free gifts should be chosen with care. They should be low cost but have a high perceived value. How you offer these gifts can also make an impact.

No other factor compares in effectiveness with curiosity.

*"Describe a gift, and some folks will want it, but more will decide they don't. But everybody wants a **secret** gift."*—Claude Hopkins

"Back-End" Sales

Once you have made a sale, you have acquired a customer. New customers are a coup, but their real value to you is after you've first sold them.

A repeat sale is almost always easier to execute than a first sale. If you have a repeat product—one that needs to be replenished regularly, this is obvious. You already know this customer buys the type of product you sell. All you need to do is motivate him to come back to buy from you. The cost of inducing this customer to repurchase a product or service is cheaper than attracting new customers. And if you can motivate this customer to return regularly, it's as if you have an annuity!

> *Tell them explicity what to do in order to purchase your product or try your service.*

But what if your product is more permanent and the customer is not likely to need or want another for a long time? Of what value, then, is a current or past customer?

This is where having a back-end product is even more important. Back-end products are items that are likely to appeal to customers who have purchased your widget. You'll want to look for and experiment with related products or services—something that will logically "fit" with your main product.

Get the names, phone numbers, and addresses of your customers. Making special offers to past and current customers by phone or direct mail is cost effective.

What if you are essentially a one-product company?

You just have to forget about the lucrative back-end business, right? *Wrong!*

Look for other merchandise, services, and companies to offer your customers. Offer to refer your customers on a percentage-of-sales basis. Or offer your mailing list to other companies on the same basis. Don't look at your list only in terms of logical extension products. The demographics or probable lifestyle of your customers may make them suitable prospects for companies offering totally unrelated products.

Reverse the process

You can do this in reverse or as a tradeoff. You can arrange to take another company's back end referrals on a percentage basis or simply trade lists. If you're not making money from your back end, you're not realizing your potential.

If you're not making money from your back end, you're not realizing your potential.

Ultimately you must generate new customers

But, of course, in order to have back-end sales, you must generate "front-end" sales—new customers. Ultimately, your business depends upon attracting new customers. Your company, like all companies, is in the business of generating new customers.

And the way to do that is to address your prospects' needs. All of your marketing efforts must focus on the targeted customer. Use specific, direct headlines and ads. Attract the attention of the intended customer in your headline. Qualify the headline by specifically addressing your target group:

- *"For all men over 45 who are concerned about …"*

- *"If you want to own the best mulching mower money can buy…"*

- *"If you want to lose weight fast with no health risks…"*

- *"For intelligent readers who want to know…"*

Go on to state your proposition or offer. Then develop support for that proposition specifically. Make a complete and compelling case. Educate, inform, give facts. Tell your prospects what you have done for them. Give your prospective customers reasons why they should buy from you. State the reasons in terms of benefits. Last of all, tell the prospect specifically how to act, exactly what he must do to obtain your product.

Make it easy, make it fun

"I am the world's worst salesman. Therefore I must make it easy for people to buy."—F.W. Woolworth

> **Your company, like all companies, is in the business of generating new customers.**

Even if you are the world's greatest salesman, make it easy to do business with you. Make it pleasant. Make it fun. Don't force your customers to jump hurdles to buy your product. Plan. Make it as easy as possible. Tell them how to do it—every step. Don't make them guess. And follow up. Establish a complete and concerted follow-up procedure. Make it easy for your customers to continue to do business with you.

A challenge

Effective marketing is a challenge to the best of us. It depends on vision, creativity, a sense of timing, an ability to spot key trends, passion, and focus. Above all you must focus—on your customer, on customer satisfaction.

Testing and analyzing

"Everything from generating new customers to reselling current and past customers hinges upon recognizing and satisfying your customers' needs—giving them what they want. The only way to find out what the marketplace wants is by testing one approach against another. Since all you ever risk is the modest cost of conservative testing, you owe it to yourself to attempt all sorts of fresh marketing applications."—Jay Abraham, *The Abraham File*

Effective marketing is *dynamic* marketing.

Chapter 5

Marketing Policies

Strengthening your marketing policies

Efficient marketing depends upon aiming at achieving an enhanced competitive position. It depends on strengthening your marketing policies in order to:

- Eliminate unprofitable or low-margin stock or services

- Optimize and target your customer base

- Stimulate customer loyalty and repeat business

In other words, you need to look at product mix, customer mix, and after-sale service.

"You cannot be all things to all people. You can please all of the people some of the time and some of the people all of the time, but you cannot please all of the people all of the time."

The above quote, attributed to another "Abraham," is so-often repeated that it has become one of the most deeply engrained clichés in our minds. None other than Abraham Lincoln was credited as being the author of those words. The question is, how do you apply Abe's observation to your business? Truly, you cannot be all things to all people. If you try, you will succeed in merely squandering your resources. The key to efficient marketing is to identify the market

> **You cannot be all things to all people. If you try, you will succeed in merely squandering your resources.**

75

segments that offer the greatest opportunity and then focus on them. Go for pleasing some of the people all of the time.

Identifying your optimum focus

First, define your market geographically. Is your business local, regional, national, global? Then define your customers. Are they upscale or budget individuals or are they retailers, chains, or wholesalers? Define your product by pricing scale—high-end, midrange, low-end, and by quality.

Examine your marketing policies

Now begin examining your marketing policies considering your product mix, customer mix, and after-sale service. Identify and exploit your areas of greatest opportunity, select which policies to pursue, and incorporate them into your marketing plan.

Optimizing product mix with product additions

Most companies sell more than one product. Optimizing product mix involves choosing the best and most profitable products for your market and volume.

Choose products with an eye toward compatibility and enhancement. New products should be compatible with your existing line. Ideally, they will actually enhance the marketability of your entire line. Let's say your line now consists of nutrition and health books that you're marketing by direct mail. You want to expand your line, and you have a chance at the latest detective novel. Now this novel would "fit" with direct mail marketing—but would it fit with your current product line and market segment? Under the circumstances, a detective novel would not enhance your present offering. And

Identify and exploit your areas of greatest opportunity.

chances are it would not be a good fit with your market segment, either. Although the book may have possibilities, it would probably require a separate mailing and a new approach. You will incur a lot of expenses that will cut into your profits and detract resources from promoting the rest of your line. In such a case you will lose focus (and, in all likelihood, money).

On the other hand, an exercise book or a "cooking for health" book would be a fit all the way around. It could complement your line and your market segment. In fact, it could enhance your current offer. And it could be added to any of the mailings you have planned without incurring a great amount of new expense. You can remain focused. And your profits will be optimized.

Or let's say you're retailing upscale clothing and are considering adding footwear to your product mix. Good idea? Perhaps. But look for an upscale line of shoes. Budget footwear probably will not appeal to your present market segment. Staying within your market segment will keep your marketing focused and efficient. Whatever your business may be, always select new products or services to complement your existing line. Ask yourself, *"Does this product 'fit' my marketing style, my product line, my pricing structure, and my market segment?"* If you must answer "no" to any of these questions, it is likely that the new product will not bring you profits.

Optimizing product mix with product subtractions

In most companies, 80 percent of the profits come from about 20 percent of the products. Why? Because things change. You add new products as market conditions change. But you never quite get around to deleting the "old" products. They don't sell very well anymore, but there is always some call for them. And as long as they are selling even a little you're making some money on them, right?

But have you considered the benefits of deleting them? Perhaps the "little" profit you're generating is less than you thought. By deleting the poorly-selling items or services, you should be able to cut the expenses of materials and supplies required to handle them. The selling expenses for this dead wood will also be cut. Internal storage space will be opened up. The time your people spend on handling these items will be freed up. You will then be able to redirect these resources to present higher margin products and possible high margin additions.

Cutting products or services can be a bit scary. Total sales will probably drop for a time. But if the products did not add to the company's overall profit and the costs of handling them are deleted along with the product, deleting them should have no adverse affect on profits. In fact, as you redirect your resources to greater focus and begin to add new high margin products, your overall profits should soar.

Optimizing Customer Mix

Selling to knowledgable customers nearly always increases your business success. Most knowledgable customers are willing to pay better for quality, efficiency, and after-sale service. Loyalty is easier to establish and you're more likely to enjoy repeat sales. A knowledgable customer is far less likely to assume that low-priced merchandise or service represents a bargain.

Selling to knowledgable customers nearly always increases your business success.

Where do you find these knowledgable customers?

An uneducated customer isn't a smart customer. He or she will typically purchase what appears to be the lowest-price product among competing merchandise, because the only knowledge he has on which to base his purchase decision is the low price. A hardware store owner I know commented on people buying hammers. Any carpenter or knowledgable Do-It-Yourselfer will purchase a quality, name-brand hammer; a DIY greenhorn, on the other hand, will purchase the cheapest hammer on the display, not suspecting that it is poorly balanced and poorly faced, which results in more bent nails. It's also made of the very cheapest, most brittle steel, so that the first or second time he attempts to remove a large nail, one of the claws is likely to break off. No bargain. You can educate a customer such as this, and help to make him a loyal customer in the process—you protect him from his own lack of knowledge, you gain a loyal customer, and it's a win-win situation! As a part of your marketing policy, you teach and educate. You tell him about your product or service, give him reasons for your pricing, tell him why delivery is delayed. If you communicate this knowledge—verbally, through your ads, with your flyers, with shelf cards, with know-ledgable and trained personnel, in every appropriate (and cost-effective) way that you can, he's much more likely to become a loyal, regular customer. And he's much more likely to tell his friends about the superior service he gets from your company.

When a buyer understands that your product is of high-quality, better-made materials, handmade, more durable—he can justify spending more for the better merchandise (or service). Similarly, when your customers understand your overstocked condition or manufacturers' discount, they understand and trust your low prices. When they know the truck didn't arrive on time, they understand delivery problems. When they know they are not being ripped off, they become loyal customers.

So to a large extent you do not merely ATTRACT smart customers, you CREATE them. Educating is part of your job of optimizing your customer base. But you must also identify the market segments that offer the greatest opportunity and then focus on them.

Concentrate on your customers who generate the highest margin per product sold.

For example, let's say that you are selling to private retailers, chain retailers, and wholesalers. Determining which class of customer brings you the highest margin cannot be done by merely looking sales volume. It's looking at associated selling costs as well.

Assuming production costs are the same, some questions for you to examine are:

- How much volume does each class generate?
- Which customer class is willing to pay the highest price?
- How much expense is attributable to selling to each class?
- What are the delivery expenses involved for each class?

Volume, of course, must be considered. However, you must determine the real profit margin for each class of customer. Only then can you decide which are your most valuable customers and how you can optimize your profits by concentrating your resources.

Can you improve profits by concentrating your resources on just high-margin customer? Or would shifting away from one type of

You must determine the real profit margin for each class of customer.

customer and concentrating on expanding geographically with the other types be more profitable?

The answers to these questions should help you decide on a policy to optimize customer mix.

After-sale customer service

In the highly-competitive business climate today, after-sale customer service is increasingly important. Efficient after-sale service stimulates customer loyalty and repeat business as well as attracting new customers.

After-sale service differs with the type of business. It might be in the form of carry-out or free delivery. Technical training or telephone support is popular with highly-technical products. Free or low-cost repair service is a familiar customer service. A flexible return policy, a money-back guarantee, and special sales promotions should also be a part of your after-sale service.

Try some unusual tactics

For example, I know of a grocery store that offered free knife sharpening in its meat department on specified days. A hardware store also offered free knife and saw sharpening and reaped free newspaper publicity as well as increased business. If yours is a small company, offering more or better after-sale services is very important. It's an efficient way to encourage your customer base to repeat business. Also, happy customers attract new customers by spontaneous word-of-mouth advertising. After-sale service is usually is an inexpensive and effective marketing tool for stimulating customer loyalty, repeat business, and even new customers.

Chapter 6

Swimming With the Currents

Having a thorough, solid marketing plan is one thing, one *big* thing. But putting that plan into work within the wider reality of the world is another. No matter what kind of business or service you would like to pilot to your personal fortune, you will be making that journey within environmental (we're talking about the sociological, political, demographic, economic and business environments) conditions that sort of encompass you do and affect your every action in significant ways.

What the sam heck am I talking about? *Trends*. **Listen:**

"The odds favoring any business plan's success can be increased if it's designed to either 1) hitch a free ride on one of the great trends rolling across the (global) economy, or 2) avoid being crushed by their awesome power. The trend from an industrial to an information economy, as we know, is closing down steel mills... while opening up knowledge-intensive industries."
—Carter Henderson in his book *Winners*

Surf or swim

The Information Age is upon us like a tidal wave. To survive, business has two choices—surf or swim out of the way. If we don't want to be crushed by it, we can't ignore it. We must take it into consideration in our planning.

> **The information age is upon us like a tidal wave.**

Great fortunes have been made riding the crest of the waves of trends. And the first waves, the biggest waves, provide the wildest rides. Great fortunes have also been lost by ignoring megatrends, by failing to adjust policies and marketing techniques.

Opportunities come and go

Some people are lucky enough to profit by piling into the surf before the waves tame down to a gentle lapping along the shore. They adjust their business plans and become millionaires by riding the big initial waves of the megatrends.

First there was the agricultural economy. Then a megatrend ushered-in the new economy of the Industrial Revolution. Some people became millionaires virtually overnight. Where did the Rockefeller fortune come from? It was accumulated by recognizing an economic trend and cashing in on it. John Davison Rockefeller was an accountant who rode the wave of the industrial revolution to riches.

The information economy

Now a new megatrend is ushering-in the information economy. This is your opportunity to profit from one of the most powerful megatrends in history. It's your turn to ride a wave to fortune. The opportunity is here. It will continue to grow for years to come; the time for you to catch the wave is now.

How can you profit from today's information economy?

*"Just in the last few years the entire information industry has grown at **twice the rate of the GNP!** We've entered the 'Information Age.' People are hungry for information and are willing to pay top dollar*

A new megatrend is ushering-in the information economy...

for it. For entrepreneurs savvy enough to jump on this booming market right now, the profit opportunities in the months ahead are nothing short of mind-boggling."—Business Opportunities Digest

Benefitting from the boom

The obvious way to benefit from the "inkformation" boom is to get into the information marketing business. Sell books, reports, cassette tapes, videotapes, computerized data (*e.g.* CD-ROMs), newsletters, home study courses, classes, seminars, and other information products.

"Information and training in the U.S. today is an $8 billion–plus industry—twice as big as the personal computer market. Its growth rate is remarkable; many of the top firms are growing at at rate of 30%–50% annually; the prospects are favorable for this growth to continue through the rest of this decade! As if that weren't enough, it's a wide-open market, too. No single company—or even group of companies—dominates the field. It's so highly fragmented that there's room for hundreds, even thousands, of new suppliers."— Don Schrello, Ph.D., *Schrello Direct Marketing Seminars*

The future of your product

Of course, there are plenty of non-information articles for sale out there generating cash flow. But don't get crushed under the force of the megatrend. Take a good, long, hard look at the future of your product or service. Will it ride-out the changes in our economy? Is it time to change your product line?

The single most important trend to understand is the changing ratio between goods and information. This change can determine whether

...This is your opportunity to profit from one of the most powerful megatrends in history.

your present employer will be in business a decade from now. If you own a business, it will determine whether your company will grow or shrink.It can determine whether your chosen study or career will be rewarded or ignored in the future. It can determine the chances of success of products and services in the marketplace, whether your wages will be likely to go up or down in the coming years, and where, how and when to invest.

Why settle for survival?

Perhaps the future for your product or service looks satisfactory to you. Wonderful! But, why settle for survival? Is your business positioned to take full advantage of the trend and boom? How about looking for opportunity? Ride the wave! Profit from the megatrend!

Enhance your profits

If there's a future in your merchandise or service, I'm certainly not advocating dumping it to ride the wave. I'm talking about using the information megatrend to augment your business and your profits.

In this, the Information Age, people will pay handsomely for the information they need. This is a very new and lucrative field.

Add information products

Consider adding information products to your present business.

If you have a gift shop, for instance, you could do seminars. Show how to make some of the craft items you probably handle. Run the seminars yourself or bring in experts.

Information is a very new and lucrative field.

Make videos or reports of the seminars and sell them. You don't have to limit yourself to the local area. Sell them by mail-order, as well.

Almost anyone can crank out a homemade video with today's technology. One of my clients did.

Dr. Max Harry is a retired veterinarian. He produced a homemade video demonstrating what to do in an emergency to save your dog's life. He had seen too many dogs brought in too late to be helped. He knew a few basic animal first-aid techniques applied immediately could have saved many of them. But their owners didn't know how.

So Harry made the video to show them how. I helped him get lots of free publicity and soon he got reviewed by a film critic! Max was asked to appear on TV. In his retirement, Max is making money and having a great time!

Books are extraordinary informational products, and books get reviews just like movies. That's one of the reasons they're such great products. What is a review if not free publicity?

Does a book seem like an ambitious undertaking to you? Is it intimidating or unappealing, outside of your area of interest? Then put your knowledge into home-study courses or seminars or reports. Or publish a newsletter. You know who your competition is in your present endeavor. They are your prospective *customers* for an industry newsletter! You could profit dearly from your competition! Now that's sweet success!

Sell an idea

Many, many business lend themselves to information marketing with just a little imagination.

"You can sell an idea or a plan; a way to do something better, or faster, or cheaper. There are a lot more people who got rich selling cookbooks than running restaurants."—Joe Karbo in his book *The Lazy Man's Way to Riches*

You think your business doesn't lend itself to information marketing? Look again! Information is one of the best products you can promote. It's compatible with nearly any business. Write a "How to." If nothing else, you would be in a position to write a "How to run my kind of business." A book or report or audiotape is often merely a compendium of ideas, experience from life, or the wisdom of others.

"People want to know 'How to' and 'Where to' and they will pay well to find it. The information industry, the production and distribution of ideas and information as opposed to goods and services, now amounts to over one-half of the gross national product. This 'dream product' is the packaging and marketing of information."—Dan Poynter, in *The Self-Publishing Manual*

"How to do it and self-help books are very popular... mail-order operators who specialize in selling bits of education can produce very profitable and satisfactory results. Further, it is an easy way to get started and is one of the most profitable areas of mail-order selling. There is a large number of such one-man enterprises in this country which are paying their owners far more than a comfortable

living." U.S. Government Publication *Establishing and Operating a mail-order Business*

Hire a writer

You don't care to write? Hire a writer. Provide the ideas and pay someone to make a product from it. Seem strange? Hiring someone to produce a product was among the best traditions of the industrial age. Why not employ this tradition in today's information age?

"Although we continue to think we live in an industrial society, we have in fact changed to an economy based on the creation and distribution of information."—John Naisbitt in his book *Megatrends*

Information distribution

But the information you market doesn't have to originate with your company. Perhaps you are engaged in distributing a product right now. With your knowledge of marketing and distribution and with a little adjustment, perhaps you could add information distribution to your business.

There are hundreds of good books that have gone out of print because of poor marketing. Consult *Books in Print*, a reference manual you can find at your library reference desk. Look for a book (about a suitable topic) that has gone out of print. Contact the author and sign the rights to publish the book. Or find an information broker. The business of an information broker is providing informational products to information distributors. There is a wide array of informational products available.

Drop-shipping

Through brokers, you can stock products to fill orders or you can make arrangements for drop-shipping. With drop-shipping, the broker stocks the inventory, not you. When you get an order from a customer, you keep your share of the money and forward the rest to the broker to pay for the product. You also enclose your shipping label addressed to the customer. The broker uses your label to ship out the product to the customer for you. Some brokers drop-ship, some don't. Ask your broker about it.

The information trend's impact on advertising

Information marketing is not the only way to take advantage of the information trend in business.

The information megatrend has also had a major impact on advertising. In this information age, people want to be "with it," up-to-the minute. Everyone wants to be an insider. Folks want to be knowledgable—they want to learn. If you offer good, useful information in your ads, you'll likely have a receptive audience. If you make an effort to educate your readers, you'll grab their attention.

Words are effective

This is the reason "editorial ads" have become so popular (for the record, print editorial ads are referred to as "advertorials"; similar broadcast ads (radio & TV) are called "infomercials"). Have you noticed how there are so many advertisers are employing them? It's a proven concept. Studies show that editorial matter gets as much as five times as much readership as advertising.

If you offer good, useful information in your ads, you'll likely have a receptive audience.

Aesthetics is losing its importance. Words are effective—honest, straightforward words. A reader or viewer wants information that he or she can use. He or she wants the whole story, the truth, the facts—compelling, irresistible reasons to buy your product.

Because these ads have the appearance of editorials, a person is drawn to them. If the ad also contains useful and/or timely information, the reader will stay with it to the end. He will believe an editorial more readily than advertising. With an editorial look, a person will be more disposed to suspend skepticism and listen to what you have to say. These editorial-style ads are well tested and demonstrated to produce results.

Incorporate welcome information into your ads

Even if you don't care to use advertorials or infomercials, exploiting the public's hunger for information can be incorporated into your advertising. Put useful hints and ideas in your ads. A repair shop owner can put basic car care hints in his ad. He might give some hints on how to get a car started on a cold morning, what detrimental effects high oil viscosity, worn spark plugs, *et al.,* exert upon an engine's starting efficiency.

Too basic? Remember, you're an expert. A lot of folks are not, and they don't know the things you take for granted. What are basics to you is valuable information to them.

If you regularly include useful information in your ads, people will appreciate it. They will read your ads and may even begin looking for them. And that's why you pay for ads—so people will read them.

Exploiting the public's hunger for information can be incorporated into your advertising.

"I believe that… the information industry will be the most dynamic and exciting sector of the U.S. economy, with tremendous opportunities for all of us."—Charles Moritz, President of Dun and Bradstreet Corporation (from a speech delivered at the Information Industry Association's annual convention)

Great fortunes can be made riding the crest of the trend or lost by failing to adjust policies and marketing techniques.

Hitch a ride

Don't be crushed by by this new wave of information. Employ it to your own advantage! Take it into consideration in your business decisions. Hitch a ride on the wave!

This is your opportunity to profit from one of the most powerful megatrends in history. Your opportunity is here. Grab it!

Chapter 7

Marketing with Imagination

Price cutting

Perhaps the most widely-used marketing ploy is price cutting. Nearly any business can lower its prices to below the competitions' and attract price-conscious buyers. This can be an effective measure when selling yourself out of trouble—such as an overstock of seasonal merchandise or a temporary cash-flow problem. But what do you gain in the long term if you don't attract enough additional business to make up the loss in margin? And what have you gained if the competition retaliates with price reductions of its own? Price-cutting is perhaps the least creative method of increasing your sales. It can be quite effective in the short run, but in the long run can be counter-productive.

Buckets of money

In the past pouring more money into advertising has been the answer to increased business. The theory was that buckets of advertising money would reap buckets of increased revenue.

New businesses were expected to earmark a large portion of their budget to advertising. Businesses were often counselled to throw as much money as possible into advertising. Successful businesses with growth in mind poured more money into advertising.

Price-cutting is perhaps the least creative method of increasing your sales.

Today's competition

Today's competition is intense, and conventional advertising can be very expensive. There are a million products and services out there clamoring for attention. Some larger companies spend more than your firm's entire net worth in just one month's advertising budget!

What can you do? How can your product get attention without overspending your budget? How can you compete with companies that have such financial resources to put into their advertising?

Buckets of money is not the answer. To be a success in business, be daring, be different, be a pioneer. In today's business climate, *imaginative* marketing is more vital than ever. Merely pouring buckets of money into advertising never guarantees commensurate (or even favorable) results.

The key is innovation

Innovation. Imagination. Many successful entrepreneurs adopt an imaginative marketing approach—an unconventional, creative, low-cost approach popularly known as "guerrilla marketing."

Guerrilla Marketing

The methods of this guerrilla marketing vary considerably. But it can be defined by its tactics and objectives.

Guerrilla marketing is:

(1) Using low-cost, unusual tactics to gain attention.

(2) Gaining maximum results from each advertising dollar.

(3) Setting your wares or services apart from the competition in the minds of your prospective customers.

> *In today's business climate, imaginative marketing is more vital than ever.*

As you can see, guerrilla marketing isn't significantly different from conventional, results-oriented marketing in what it strives to achieve.

The difference is in the tactics

It's rather like comparing guerrilla and conventional warfare—the difference is in the tactics.

Guerrilla marketing uses the unusual, the innovative, to gain attention and stand out from the rest. It's a matter of seeing the possibilities in new and unorthodox approaches. It's looking at the little things as well as the big, with a new eye. It's being different, thinking creatively.

Creative marketing through creative thinking

Right. But how do you achieve creative thinking. How do you come up with these innovative ideas?

"Creative thinking may mean simply the realization that there's no particular virtue in doing things the way they've always been done."—Rudolf Flesch

Okay, so you accept the fact that the conventional way may not be the only way—or even the best way. But, still, how do you come up with a new and different way?

Are you scratching your head thinking, or is it just a case of dandruff?

You must become a creative thinker—so you'll probably need to change the way you think.

You must become a creative thinker, so you'll probably need to change the way you think.

95

Becoming aware of the process

To learn to be a creative thinker, you must become aware of the process, of what you do and what you seek to accomplish when you engage your thought processes.

The first step to awareness is to recognize that you use *two types* of thinking; I know some people who don't use even *one* type, but you and I, of course, use two. Edward de Bono, an expert on thinking, labels them *vertical* and *lateral* thinking.

Taking logical steps down the garden path

Vertical thinking is "conventional" thinking—the kind we are most familiar with because we employ it most often. This is the logical, step-by-step approach that assists you in choosing the what you initially perceive to be the most appropriate path to the solution of your problem. And it requires you to make a judgement of right or wrong at each step of that path.

As you can see, vertical thinking takes only logical, structured paths. It can shut off pathways or ideas right at the entrance gate. And at any step along the way, you might make a judgement that slams a gate, shutting off further exploration in that direction. Logic is wonderful, but sometimes what works may be contrary to what seems obvious or logical.

Skipping blithely down the garden path

Lateral thinking, on the other hand, suspends judgement and approaches ideas with humor, insight and creativity. It goes tripping down unlikely paths, exploring and speculating, unafraid to

Lateral thinking approaches ideas with humor, insight and creativity.

experiment with the unusual and bizarre. It looks at alternatives. It explores paths that may seem irrelevant.

"There is a correlation between the creative and the screwball. So we must suffer the screwball gladly."—Kingman Brewster

Lateral thinking takes you off the beaten path and may lead you to an insight, a new and innovative concept, or a restructuring of the problem itself. It closes no gates. You can see that lateral thinking opens the way to innovative and unusual ideas.

Throwing logic to the winds

Hold it! I'm not advocating throwing logic to the winds—just suspending it on occasion. You need to employ both types of the thought process: *Lateral* thinking helps you to generate new ideas; *vertical* thinking enables you to develop these concepts into workable methods. In other words, spread your creative thinking process laterally (left and right) as you develop new ideas, then center on the promising ideas and develop them vertically.

Be a screwball. Get crazy. Go beyond the obvious. Suspend your judgement of new methods and approaches as you explore the possibilities of ideas that may seem outlandish or preposterous. Imagine some seemingly foolish ideas and follow them through in your mind.

Six foot peanut?

How about dressing someone up in a human-sized peanut? Foolish? Perhaps, but it's been done with great results! The people who met the "peanut" and got a free sample right from his hot little hand

Lateral thinking helps you to generate new ideas; vertical thinking enables you to develop these concepts into workable methods.

will tell you this method stood out from the rest! A peanut doesn't fit with your product? Well, if a peanut can parade around in the parking lot and shake hands with people, why can't your gadget?

Brainstorming

Still doesn't work? Then sit down and "brainstorm" ideas. Do it alone or make it a party. Group brainstorming can be very effective. Organize a brainstorming session with family, colleagues, employees, friends, just to generate ideas that otherwise might never be generated. Don't dilute your brainstorming session by entering into a lengthy discussion or critique of each suggestion introduced; just quickly jot down each one and go on to the next newly-spawned idea in non-judgemental fashion. Detailed analytical discussion must come later, when the brainstorming has concluded.

Think this is just a nutty waste of time? Think again.

You've heard of the "think tanks"—the groups of brains that are paid megabucks to come up with ideas? "Brainstorming" is how they work. They know that ideas can build. Sometimes the preposterous ideas lead directly to great new concepts. And sometimes just getting the preposterous out of the way opens the door to new insights.

Don't toss away illogical ideas

Lateral thinking doesn't require that you make an effort to be silly—just that you don't toss away ideas that seem outlandish at first glance. Write them down and follow them where they go. Don't make judgements that will slam the gates on further exploration.

Group brainstorming can be very effective.

Don't be afraid to think about something strange and different. Thinking about it won't cost much! And this kind of thinking—audacious, creative—leads to effective new concepts that stand out from the rest.

Jerry Wilson, inventor of the *Soloflex*™ exercise machine, is a maverick. A very successful maverick. Before his success with *Soloflex*, Wilson was a charter jet pilot flying "high-rollers" to Las Vegas. After observing his wealthy passengers, he noted, *"It didn't seem they were smarter than any of us, but they knew something; I found out it was audacity."*

Imagination, enthusiasm and **audacity**—the cobblestones of Wilson's road to success.

Simple ideas can seem silly but be effective

Sometimes simple ideas can seem silly. Yet simple things, such as a change in packaging design, can work wonders.

Is everyone in the field boxing the product? So what? It's been done that way for the past 300 years? So what? Then maybe a bag or a bubble pak will catch the attention of the consumer. Can't be done? Why not?

If it truly must be in a box, then can the box be made of plastic, wood, metal, glass? And the shape? Need it be square or rectangular? Why not a star or a mouse shape? And the color? Why has it never been boxed in pink? Or stripes? Or plaid? Too elementary? No way! Nothing is too simple if it works.

Imagination, enthusiasm and audacity—the cobblestones of the road to success.

99

A small "niche company" that I know of decided to market a healthy snack. They positioned themselves as a healthy snack that tastes good. Their successful innovative marketing procedures centered around their packaging. They used a distinctive package that proclaimed the health and taste benefits of their product. Simple? Yes. Effective? Very.

This company used marketing innovations all the way. They reinforced package recognition with the "peanut man" idea. People, dressed in human sized snack bags, handed out free samples to the spectators at large public events.

In vans painted in their distinctive package colors, they went to beaches, races, wherever people gathered. They entertained consumers with skits and jokes and handed out samples.

Foolish? Perhaps. But they got package recognition and taste trials in one shot! And at a relatively low cost. Later, confronted with the multitude of products on the snack shelves in the grocery stores, consumers found one distinctively different package that offered a guilt-free and tasty product.

"Hey!" they said to themselves, *"That's the package that goofy guy was dressed in. You know, the sample was really tasty, and it's good for you, too. Why not purchase that one?"*

Recognition. It works.

In the highly-competitive snackfood market, this little company carved out a profitable slice of the business! Simple and low-cost tactics like these can be very effective.

Make the giveaway a memorable event

Give away free samples. A certain percentage of those who sample your merchandise will probably become your customers. But don't just hand out the samples. Do it with flair. Drop them from airplanes. Deliver them by balloon. Entertain, sing. It's show biz. Entertainment time. Generate excitement. Attract attention. Give the consumers something to remember. Make the giveaway a memorable event, and you'll gain customers. In addition, you'll gain a lot of valuable word-of-mouth advertising.

Public events

Can't afford to sponsor big public events? Ask to come in as a second- or third-level sponsor. If you can generate a little entertainment and give away some samples, you might get a low-level sponsorship at little or no cost.

Contingency giveaways

Make a giveaway contingent on a donation to specific charities. Offer free merchandise in return for a minimum donation. Do it with style, with show.

How about a public challenge to other businesses in your area? Something such as: If you give a $200 to this charity, I'll donate $200 in product to your favorite charity (retail value, of course, but your challenge need not specify that). This would work well if your product is something the charity can use itself or sell or offer as prizes for donations.

Or you could go directly to a charity and offer to help set up a donation-for-a-prize scheme. They run the program, you donate the prizes. Whatever advertising of the contest they do will get your product name before the public and give you a caring image.

Or just give some product to a charity with the understanding that they will sell it at a discounted price that you specify. They keep all the proceeds, you benefit from a "caring" image, and your samples are distributed to prospective future customers.

Give free merchandise to other companies to sell or give away with their products. Remember the detergent and clothes washer combination? If you are the detergent, you get an implicit referral from the maker of the washer and the benefits of free sampling.

Can't afford to hire sales reps to distribute your product? How about giving free product to sales reps to sell at a discounted price? Let the rep keep the proceeds as payment for distribution. The first round of profits go to the rep, but the reorders come to you.

This method can be used with advertisers, too. Give them product to sell in exchange for publicity. Or pay for advertising with product that they can use for prizes. Or offer a percent-of-sales deal.

Giveaways do not have to be samples

You know the common joke about waiting for the children to come home to program the VCR? It points up the sad fact that your prospective customer may have only a vague idea how to use a product he or she would like to own.

Often customers are not getting the full benefit of a product. Give your customers free reports or seminars or videos on how to use your product. Knowing they will be able to make full and correct use of a product, customers will be more disposed to buy.

If most of your competition is not offering this benefit, you'll have a great advantage. This has been used very effectively by some computer software merchants.

Training programs are valuable to the consumer. They don't have to be free as long as you charge less than your competitor charges.

Training programs generally don't cost a bundle to implement and are almost guaranteed to increase sales.

Conventional advertising can seem innovative

Methods of promoting individual products have become traditional. It's predictable. You know what to expect in TV and radio commercials and the print media ads—soap, cars, cereals, *et al.* Direct mail also has its traditional products to sell. Assorted retail outlets sell certain products.

So conventional wisdom dictates how you will sell your particular wares. It's all laid out there for you because this is the way it's done, right? Wrong.

To stand out from the others, you need to try new ways of selling. Perhaps your innovative approach will simply be to use a conventional method of marketing—except that is not conventional for your product. Has your product always been sold by direct mail? Well, why can't it be sold through TV or radio commercials? Who says you can't ignore the rules of convention?

The fact is, many companies are doing just that. Traditional

Who says you can't ignore the rules of convention?

methods are becoming less effective—probably because the "same old, same old" is boring the consumers.

So when they see unexpected products being promoted in direct mail or on TV, they wake up and say, *"Hey, this is different."* They take notice.

Sometimes old fashioned seems innovative

In this rapidly-changing world, occasionally an old-fashioned idea seems new and creative.

A firm I know of uses a combination of the old fashioned and new technology. It educates its consumers through television commercials employing a down-home style. In addition, the firm's twice-yearly sales are never advertised. They rely totally entirely on word-of-mouth. Yet they draw large crowds—bigger crowds with each event. All on old-fashioned, inexpensive word-of-mouth!

Besides seeming creative and innovative, old-fashioned has a certain appeal. It seems warm and comforting to people often feeling bewildered and left groping for an liferope in the midst of turbulent change.

We've all seen a certain homey commercial for a motel chain. What could be more old fashioned and homey than *"leaving a light on for you"*? Warm fuzzies in marketing? Of course, why not?

Bathroom stalls

One innovative concept that must have seemed pretty silly in the first analysis is advertising in public restroom stalls. I can imagine the laughter that provoked. Yet it's a novel concept. You're a

Occasionally an old-fashioned idea seems new and creative.

"captive audience." You sit there with nothing else to look at. Of course you read the ads—it's better reading than the graffiti. At least, most of the time. And what else is there to do while performing an otherwise mindless task?

Experiment

"The key to victory is to plunge into the thick of things... then see what happens."—Napoleon

Now we're back to the same old saw... *testing*. Experiment with your ideas. Change them. Experiment again. Not everything is going to be a smash. Not everything will work. The way to find out what will work is to run small, inexpensive tests. When you find something that works, proceed to test variations of the theme, making certain you alter only one variable at a time so that you know for sure what variable is changing your results. Think creatively—perhaps a combination of approaches will work best for you. In fact, you should always be testing new promotions. Even if you have a very successful approach, it will wear out sometime.

The sky's the limit...

Imaginative marketing spans from the old-fashioned to computer on-line services. The sky's the limit!

Actually even that's not even the limit —there's skywriting, hot air balloons, helicopters, even the *Fuji* and *Goodyear* blimps. All waiting in the wings (if you'll pardon the pun) to be used creatively. Go for it—the sky's *not* the limit! Think creatively. Use your imagination. You'll surprise yourself!

Go for it— the sky's NOT the limit!

Chapter 8

Generating Free Publicity

Let's talk about advertising. What is advertising anyway? Publicity! *Paid* publicity, that is. After all, advertising informs your prospective customers that you're there, what products or services you're selling, who you are, what you do. That's paid publicity. It's difficult to imagine a company succeeding without some form of publicity—your prospective customers must know you're there before they can choose to buy from you. Such publicity is worth paying for.

Peter McWilliams, author of the widely-acclaimed *The Word Processing Book*, sold over a half million copies of his self-published book in a little over a year. He earned about $5,000,000 on that little $10 book. How did he do it? In his own words, *"Publicity, publicity, publicity—and perhaps a little talent—maybe not."*

Publicity is probably the best investment you could make in your business or career; if you can get it for free, go for it?

It's a great way for a new business with little cash to invest in advertising to get a startup boost. But it doesn't have to be limited to new enterprises… shouldn't the established businesses make use of it, too? Yes, of course. But if it's free, how effective is it?

Your prospective customers must know you're there before they can choose to buy from you.

I published a newsletter called Information Marketing for several years. One of my subscribers, Harold, an airline pilot, started a small business out of his home in his spare time. His product was a book entitled *How to Make Your Paycheck Last* priced at $19.95. Harold couldn't afford to buy ads to sell his product, so he went after free publicity in newspapers and magazines.

Family Circle magazine used a small 3" x 3" news feature about him. That one little news item pulled in 181,000 orders. Anyone can see that's a lot of money! To be precise, $3,610,950. All resulting from one little news item that didn't cost Harold a dime—free publicity

But Harold was selling information products. What if you're not into information products? It doesn't matter! You can sell almost anything with free publicity. Almost anything? You bet!

Look back at one of the most bizarre products of all time: Remember the *"Pet Rock"*? If it wasn't the most unlikely consumer product of all time, it ranks right up there on the list. But Gary Dahl sold one million of those ordinary rocks and made $1 net profit on each one! And he never spent one penny on advertising! He did it through free publicity and nothing else. He simply wrote a news release and mailed it out to a lot of magazine and newspaper editors. TIME magazine gave him a half page news story. You know what he would have had to pay for a half-page advertisement in TIME? Probably tens of thousands of dollars!

Free publicity works. In fact, a half page news story probably pulls more than a half-page paid ad that costs tens of thousands of dollars. Why? Because more people read and believe news items

That one little news item pulled in 181,000 orders.

than they do advertisements. As we discussed in Chapter 5, a person tends to believe an editorial more than advertising.

Okay, but Harold and Gary got into magazines. What about newspapers?

Newspaper editors are particularly news-hungry. Their jobs demand it. They must supply fresh editorial matter every day, 365 days a year. Every day! On deadline! Of course they're news hungry.

But is free newspaper publicity effective? Think about it. When you read the newspaper do you read the ads and maybe a few eye-catching news items along the way? Just the opposite, right? You read the news and maybe a few eye-catching ads. Just like everyone else.

Here's a story about one of my clients who started out with a little 2½" by 3" news item in The *Cleveland Plain Dealer* newspaper. His product was a reproduction of an old "wedding certificate" dating from the 1800s. It has engravings of cupids and hearts, like a Valentine. It says Wedding Certificate and has spaces for the date and the names of the husband and wife.

My client and his wife had been married for fifty years. They told me their successful marriage was due in large measure to this certificate. They kept it hanging in their kitchen as a constant reminder of their love and commitment. This is exactly what I said in the news release. My client's costs were nominal. He had to pay for preparing the release, and for photocopies, envelopes and postage stamps. The *Plain Dealer* news item pulled in over $1200 dollars. It took one week from mailing the release to collecting $1200!

> **Newspaper editors are news-hungry. Their jobs demand it.**

My client was ecstatic and began reinvesting the income into mailing more releases. The money just kept coming in. Multiply that $1200 income by just 100 newspapers. He could make well over $100,000! All on free publicity!

Newspaper publicity can snowball rapidly. Start out with one newspaper story and keep the process going—story after story, paper after paper. Another man I know of did this until he achieved sales of over $2 million in his first year!

In addition, you may soon begin receiving calls from large mail-order catalog houses! My client with the wedding certificate did. They saw his news stories and they became interested, too!

Once you get the publicity and your product is selling well, mail-order catalogs want your product. Just show them your clippings and sales records, and they'll be interested!

And think of this. Even if your product flops in a major catalog, you'll still sell thousands of dollars worth of your product or service. Big companies that send out millions of catalogs need thousands of units of your merchandise to cover the orders they receive even if it's a flop by their standards! You won't make as much profit per unit as you do selling direct since you'll be selling wholesale, but properly done you'll make it up on volume. And how simple it is! Instead of mailing out hundreds of orders, you need send only one large shipment, and you deposit only one large check!

Free radio publicity works too, and fast! One of my clients wrote a booklet on how to meet the love of your life. While it was still unpublished—just a stack of typed pages—I advised him to phone

> **Newspaper publicity can snowball rapidly. Start out with one newspaper story and keep the process going.**

some local radio talk shows. One put him on the air that day. Throughout the interview my client kept giving out his order desk phone number; in fact, it was the number of the answering service he'd hired just that morning. The phones just kept ringing!

How would you like to make $6,000 in your first two hours and at zero financial risk? My client did risk the 25 cents for the phone call! Once the money came in, he used some of it to run off copies of his report at his local copy shop.

Radio talk show interviews are an easy and effective way to promote your wares or services. They are handled over the telephone so you don't even have to leave home. And you can reach many different radio audiences all over the U.S. in a single day!

The best day for a news release to arrive at your local radio station is Monday. It seems Sunday is a "slow" news day and stations are understaffed on weekends, so not too much gets prepared for the next week. Announcers will appreciate it when they come in on Monday facing a paucity of news and find your interesting item waiting to be read on the morning newscast.

News releases written for radio should suggest timeliness by including references to dates in the near future. Radio is a fast-paced medium and you want to grab the attention of listeners with an issue or an event that is going to affect them right now.

Free publicity often brings in more than paid advertising brings in. Even if it pulls less than an ad, it's still a winner because it's free! You've incurred no advertising expense.

Even if free publicity pulls less than an ad, it's still a winner because it's free!

You may be wondering why the media would want to run your story. Remember, the media is always looking for news stories. News editors need good news items. News is the product that they sell. They pay reporters to go out and find news item; you're giving away that product free! Why wouldn't they be interested?

However, you can't simply go storming into a news editor's office and demand free publicity. The secret to successfully using this strategy is in knowing how to approach the editors. The best approach is by mail. Send your story in the form of a news release written in a newsy, journalistic style. Include a sharp, 4" x 6" or 5" x 7" glossy photo of your product, if possible. Some items are difficult for editors to describe; a good photo can help to induce the editor to use your press release, and the photo will help to draw the readers' attention to your article. Make sure it's a good, clear, sharp photograph that will reproduce well. If it will be reproduced in black & white, then send a top-quality b&w photo. If you expect that it might be reproduced in color, include a 35mm color transparency (slide) as well.

Okay, news is the media's business, but they aren't in the business of giving away ad space. So why would they include your address and ordering information in a writeup of your product?

One reason is that publishers want you to make money; they're hoping you will get a good response so that you'll come back and run an ad. If you come up a winner, you might continue to run paid ads for years. Another reason editors include your address and ordering information is because it's the media's function to inform their readers about interesting people, products, services, and events.

Also, they often include the information on how to contact you simply to avoid being bugged by readers who want the information. Busy news offices don't have time to field hundreds of calls and letters asking how to contact you or place an order.

But there are no guarantees that the ordering information will be included in the news item. None at all. Ordering information could be left out for any number of reasons that you can't control, including somebody is having a bad day.

There are a couple of facts to consider, though, to increase your chances of having the information included in the news story.

If you sound too commercial they'll leave it out—not run the item at all. So make it newsy and don't hype it like a snake oil sales pitch. A good approach is to matter-of-factly include the information without the *"Call now..."* and the *"But wait, there's more..."* approach.

It also pays to know a little about how news stories are handled. Have you ever thought about how they get everything to fit perfectly in the space they have? Well, if editorial matter doesn't quite fit, they begin cutting it. Usually it's shortened starting at the end and working backward.

My strategy is to try to weave the ordering information into the middle of the news story, if possible. If it's tagged on at the end, it's more likely to be cut. Be low key and stick to the facts. Be brief and newsworthy. Put the news right up front, in the very first paragraph. Just casually slip the ordering information in as part of the story.

Be brief and newsworthy. Put the news right up front, in the very first paragraph.

Editors are busy people—and under constant deadlines. Give them something they can put right into their pages without rewriting. If they don't have to rewrite it, they aren't so likely to cut anything out of the story. But offer them real news, not badly disguised advertising. Don't try a sales pitch or your release will get pitched. Editors are looking for real news, valuable, interesting information and maybe a story with a little humor. If you can offer them that, they probably won't care if it also happens to work like an ad for you.

Don't hint to the editors that you will run paid ads later if they give you some free publicity now. They may be willing to run your story if it's an interesting news item, but any hint of deal making will probably guarantee your story a place in the trash.

What if your merchandise isn't newsworthy? Not to worry. Almost every product or service can be can be turned into news if it's presented with an interesting angle.

Jeff Slutsky, author of *Streetfighting* and one of my former newsletter subscribers, told a story about how he promoted a new restaurant. He looked in the phone book and found a person named John Wayne listed. This was before *The Duke* passed away. He invited this local John Wayne to dine at his restaurant at no charge. Then he alerted the media that John Wayne would be dining at the new restaurant on Friday night. Everyone showed up and had a good laugh and a good time. It could have backfired, of course. But Jeff kept the mood happy (and the drinks flowing, no doubt). He received a ton of free television airtime, too.

How's that for free publicity? Was his promotion newsworthy? With his unique angle, it was!

Okay, so you have an interesting angle, but will the editor read it? It's the editor's job to read news releases. Almost every story submitted in a news release format will get read.

If it is composed in an upbeat, journalistic style in the manner in which a reporter or public relations professional writes, it will stand a much better chance of being printed. Remember, editors have to fill those pages every day. They're hungry for news that they can use. They're also busy. They appreciate news items they can use without a lot of copy editing. If they have to do a major rewrite, though, they might just pass it up.

What's the format do you use for your release? How do you make it look like news? It isn't too difficult.

Use plain white business letter size and quality paper.

Put the words "News Release" at the top of the page in large print so the busy media people know at a glance that it is news. Below that include the name and phone number a person the media can call for more information. At the top of the page, let the editor know if it is "For Immediate Release," or for use on a specific date, or "at will."

Next, use a headline that grabs attention and arouses interest. Leave space between the headline and first paragraph for the editor to write notes to his typesetter. Double space the body.

I have included some examples at the end of this chapter. As you will see the format is quite simple. Okay, that's the format, but how do you write a release in today's journalistic style? One that can be used without a lot of rewriting?

Use a headline that grabs attention and arouses interest.

What if you're not a writer?

Why don't you try just one double-spaced page. Even if you don't consider yourself to be a writer, you'll probably surprise yourself. Just sit down and tell your story. If you have trouble getting started, go to the library and read a dozen newspapers in one sitting. Notice how they're written in a breezy, fast-paced, tight literary style. Each word packs a punch. It's quick and simple writing—a lot of short sentences, everything right to the point. Newspapers use an-easy-to-read, terse style.

Use vibrant, fresh language and include interesting information.

Here are a few hints: Keep it short and to the point. Double-space your text. One page is best but if you run to two pages, use only one side of each page. Don't send just a list of facts, use an angle. Make it interesting, fascinating, exciting—but avoid 1930s-style hyperbole, such as *"Wow! Dr. Wozniak's Snake Oil is the talk of the nation! Millions of delighted customers use it as suntan oil, cooking oil, motor oil and salad dressing!"* Tell a story, but keep it believable.

Write it to read like a story so it can be employed as a news item. Think of how you would like to see it printed; it may end up printed word for word. Use everyday language, write it just about as you would state it verbally. No academic or scholarly language. This is not the place to exercise vocabulary skills. Do, however, use picture words—words that will conjure up pictures in the reader's mind. Say it in as few words as possible. Be clear, concise and believable in your wording. Use vibrant, fresh language and include interesting information.

Paragraphs should be kept short. Forget the old saw about one-line paragraphs; they're perfectly fine as long as they're not too long. Paragraphs of varying lengths make your copy more interesting.

As with the paragraphs, vary the length of your sentences. If you use only lengthy sentences, you will lose your reader. All short ones will bore the reader. Avoid convoluted sentences. Break them down. Make them clear and easy to read.

Rewrite and rewrite until you have a dramatic factual story with no wasted words. Eliminate words and phrases that aren't important to the story. Experiment with arrangements and words until your story is concise, interesting, and clear.

Remember, even the pros seldom sit down and write an item without doing rewrites. Rewriting is not an indication of incompetency—it's merely a step in the process.

Give it a catchy headline. When you are writing the headline, you'll want to focus upon getting attention. Look through the *National Enquirer* or in magazines such as *Reader's Digest* and other publications.

Speaking of the *Reader's Digest*, they ran some title-testing ads. Check out the titles that got top billing on the cover of each issue. These are the tested news headlines that sell. These are the headlines to emulate for your news releases.

Study the headlines that grab your attention. Why did they grab your attention? Did they make you want to read the rest of the article? Take them apart, dissect them, study them. The best way to learn is to examine what successful writers—including ad copy

Study the headlines that grab your attention. Why did they grab your attention?

writers—have done. What's being used is a good indicator of what the publications want.

What do you do if you give it your best shot, and you just can't write it? You could check out *A Short Course in Copywriting* by Victor O. Schwab (Wilshire Book Co., 12015 Sherman Rd., North Hollywood, CA 91605). This is an excellent book and one of my favorites. It lays out a tested step-by-step system for highly-profitable ads. If you don't know where to begin, you can follow this plan and turn out an ad that pulls and pulls.

If you're stuck for a headline, here you will find help. There are tips and examples on how to write your first paragraph, ways to hold interest longer, how to influence the effectiveness of your ad.

Or, try hiring a local newspaper journalist or a college journalism student to do it for you. You'll have to pay for the service, but chances are it won't be a bundle of money. You could hire a public relations firm to write news releases for you. Although this may get a little pricey, the results could be worth it. Of course, paying a large fee to have a public relations firm prepare your release rather defeats the purpose. Would you still call it free publicity?

Once you have your press release written, where do you send it? Whether you plan to start out by blitzing the publishing world or by shooting for a few winners and then pyramiding your earnings into more media channels, you need some names and addresses. Try to get the names of the editors at the publications so you can route your release to them personally.

You can go to your local library and get the information from their reference books. The use of these books is free. Some titles to look for are:

- *Bacon's Publicity Checker*

- *Broadcasting Yearbook*

- *Gebbie's All-In-One Directory*

- *Magazine Industry Marketplace*

- *National Directory of Newsletters*

- *News Bureaus in the U.S.*

- *Standard Periodical Directory*

- *Standard Rate and Data*

- *Syndicated Columnists Directory*

- *The Newsletter Yearbook Directory*

- *TV Publicity Outlets*

- *Working Press of the Nation*

And once again, don't forget to consult your library's reference librarian for his or her suggestions.

You can rent mailing lists. Look in the *Yellow Pages* under "Mailing Lists" or "Mailing List Brokers." Try to get lists with the names of editors included, not just a list of publications.

When you address your press release include the name and title of the editor. The title will ensure that your letter goes to the proper office even if the addressee has quit or been promoted.

When your news release has been published and the orders start rolling in, you'll probably be interested in how many orders each publication is bringing in. After all, free publicity is an excellent way to test the effectiveness of each magazine or newspaper before you risk investing in advertising.

To do this testing scientifically, you must begin before your press releases go out. When you type up the release, leave room for a key code in the ordering address. You might include the word "Dept." with blank space following it. Before sending it out, key it by entering an identifier in the blank. For example, the release going to *Redbook* magazine may be keyed Dept. "RB" and the one you send to TIME magazine keyed Dept. "T". The releases may be keyed by hand or you might key them by computer as they are printed. It's not a good idea to leave the key space blank for the publisher to fill-in. Although some magazines will fill it in for you, others do not. Do it yourself, to be sure it gets keyed properly.

Now when the cash starts coming in, you'll know which publications generated the orders. To make use of this information, just add up the cash income from each key code which represents each publication. Check out the size of your publicity story in each publication and then find out what they would charge for an ad of approximately the same size. Then you compare the total income from that publication to what an ad would cost to see if running an ad would be justified.

Now you know approximately what to expect from a paid ad of a similar size in each magazine that your story was published in. You can invest your advertising dollars with less risk by picking only the publications that pull the best for you.

If your story is picked up by the wire services (such as AP or UPI) or a syndicated column, it can suddenly appear in newspapers from coast to coast. This could upset your scientific testing. But the national publicity will probably offset your disappointment over the blown testing!

You can still get an idea of where the sales are coming from. If you get swamped with orders from a certain city, then your story was probably seen in that city's newspaper. That isn't very scientific, but perhaps you can sweat that detail on your way to the bank.

However, until your story gets picked up by the syndicates, using a method to test the effectiveness of each magazine or newspaper before you risk investing in paid advertising is a good, sound business practice.

Free publicity is worth pursuing. It has impact. It should be a part of every company's marketing strategy. Publicity is probably the best investment you will make in your business or career. It's difficult to imagine a company succeeding without some form of publicity— your prospective customers must first know you are there before they can choose to buy from you.

"Since that deluge of newspaper articles I have been so flooded with questions, invitations, suggestions, that I keep dreaming that I'm roasting in Hell, and the mailman is Satan eternally yelling at me, throwing more bundles of letters at my head because I have not answered the old ones."—Albert Einstein

May your news releases and articles bring you such a flood of orders! On the following four pages are samples of news releases, each one represented with a cover page and a "news flash" page.

Free publicity should be a part of every company's marketing strategy.

News Release

CONTACT: John Baptiste
Puma Publishing
1670 Coral Drive
Santa Maria, CA 93454

PHONE# (805) 925-3216

FOR IMMEDIATE RELEASE

To request a review copy
fax (805) 925-2656

FREE HELP FROM UNCLE SAM TO HELP YOU START OR EXPAND YOUR OWN SMALL BUSINESS IS WAITING FOR YOU TO CLAIM IT

SANTA MARIA, CA--Business author William Alarid is telling all--revealing little known sources of free government help for small businesses. Everything from advice, counseling services and publications, to grants, loans, loan guarantees, financial incentives and much more, all free for the asking. Alarid has written a book revealing 100 of his "secret" sources for getting free help from Uncle Sam. He gives the names, addresses and details on government sources that specialize in small business assistance.

"Many small businesses are eligible for free assistance, services, even loans, and grants," says Alarid, "but they have no idea how or where to find this free help. Uncle Sam offers everything from advice to assistance for women business owners wanting to sell to NASA, to grants, loans, and financial incentives." Alarid's book *Free Help From Uncle Sam To Start Your Own Business,* is available by calling 1-800-255-5730, ext. 110, or by sending $14.95 to Puma Publishing, 1670 Coral Drive, Suite 31, Santa Maria, CA 93454. Included in the sources are 100 government agencies that purchase from small businesses and government programs that offer financial help, services, export assistance, publications, free help for women and minorities, loans for teenagers, special help for handicapped business owners, etc., all listed with names, addresses, telephone numbers and descriptions for easy reference.

--END--

News Release

CONTACT: John Baptiste, Mgr.
                    Puma Publishing Co.
                    1670 Coral Drive
                    Santa Maria, CA 93454

PHONE #   (805) 925-3216

FOR IMMEDIATE RELEASE

(Review copy available upon request)

Profitable Retirement

(NU)-The average American lives 19 years after retirement----time for a whole new career. If you've contemplated starting a business by recycling current skills or developing new ones after you retire, it is essential to know the pluses and the pitfalls so you can work smarter, not harder.

A new guide book, ***Retiring to Your Own Business: How You Can Launch a Satisfying, Productive and Profitable Second Career,*** can help smooth the way. It is written by Gustav Berle, who practices what he preaches, having taught college business courses and written 10 books since "retiring."

From helping you assess your options to providing step-by-step action plans, Berle outlines how to plunge into your own business without sinking financially or emotionally.

There's advice on buying businesses and franchises, setting up a home office, operating as your own bank and turning an avocation into a vocation.

Berle's book offers practical tools, including how to prepare a business plan, figure personal net worth, and get assistance from the Small Business Administration. It lists networking sources and publications, and explains how near-retirees can ward off potential disasters because of layoffs, ill health or early retirement.

A chapter of case histories gives a personal look into the lives of dozens of people who are making retirement payoff.

Berle's book ***Retiring to Your Own Business*** can be ordered with a credit card by calling 1-800-255-5730 ext. 110 or by sending $16.95 to Puma Publishing Co., 1670-R Coral Drive, Santa Maria, CA 93454. It is available in better bookstores such as Waldenbooks and Brentanos.

---END--

News Release

FOR IMMEDIATE RELEASE

CONTACT: Steffie Kulka
              S.G. Kulka Co.
              P.O. Box 37
              Warspite, Alberta
              Canada T0A 3N0

PHONE#:

YOUR "SOMETHING FOR NOTHING" IS WAITING FOR YOUR REQUEST

You've always heard that you never get something for nothing. This is a common misconception! Actually, there are many companies out there that want you to cash in on free information, product samples, recipes, and advice from experts. Most people are unaware that these opportunities exist; numerous free offers often go unpublicized and are overlooked by the general public.

Federal, state and international departments of public information offer tourist brochures, maps and travel tips. Other companies are giving away samples of lotions, seeds, iron-ons, vitamins, decals, even jewelry. Teachers can cash in on instructional aids such as posters, diagrams, charts, award certificates, and ideas for informational and interesting lectures. Available to you are countless recipe booklets, "how to" manuals, diet and fitness guides, safety and emergency first aid tips, health and beauty secrets. All free -- if you know where to look.

Two great places to look for free offers is in these booklets: *A Few Thousand of the Best FREE Things in America* and *Free Things for Kids to Write Away For*. Compiled within their bulging covers are thousands of freebees, just waiting to be discovered. The booklets cost a nominal $2.00 each, and can be requested by writing to: S.G. Kulka Co, Dept 37, Warspite, Alberta Canada T0A 3N0.

END

NEWS RELEASE

FOR IMMEDIATE RELEASE:

Contact: W.W. "Bill" Magness
               P.O. Box 5011
               Pine Bluff, AR 71611
Phone #:   (501) 534-6260

THE SECRET OF A LONG AND HAPPY MARRIAGE?

What did grandma and grandpa know about marriage that we don't? A couple from Arkansas married 53 years have some ideas on what may have made the difference back then and, they believe, may still help today.

Times have changed but couples continue to "tie the knot" in record numbers. Now however, almost as many couples later find themselves in divorce court. Are we missing something today . . . some secret ingredient that wasn't passed on over the years?

Three generations of the Magness family swear by an antique, old fashioned "Marriage Certificate" that dates back to the late 1800's. "This worked for my mom and dad and for Jewell and myself, and now for our son," says Bill Magness. A lot of other folks must agree as the requests for engravings of the Marriage Certificate are pouring in to the Magness' P.O Box 5011, Pine Bluff, Arkansas 71611.

Bill and Jewell had some printed up for wedding gifts and soon everyone wanted them. So he began to supply the demand for the 8 x 10″ size at $9 and the 16 x 20″ size at $19, or both for only $23 postage paid.

Ask Bill if business is good and he'll tell you, "It's too good. We can't keep up with it but we love every minute of it!"

Chapter 9

Direct Mail and Mailing Lists

Direct mail is more personal

We've talked about advertising. Let me say this: general advertising in any media—even if the message is addressed to a specific group—is an indirect connection. And impersonal. You can (and should) personalize it to a certain extent. Your message can be slanted to address a specific group, but it's still indirect. And it's a connection that may not even be made at all. How do you know if your customer will be at the receiving end of it? Mailing lists, on the other hand, allow you to connect directly with your prospective customers. Used properly, direct mail is personal and can bring in amazing results.

How can you use direct mail in your business?

Well, you can send out a sales letter promoting an item or service. The letter is your salesman. It is perceived as personal. You may want to include some backup material such as brochures and folders. But remember, these are not perceived as being as personal as a letter. If you are selling a book or newsletter, brochures may be a waste of money.

Form letters

A letter need not display a personalized heading to be effective. Form letters can work beautifully. But make them lively, conversational, and focused on customer benefits. On the other hand, with a modern desktop computer and software, "personalizing" forms letters is not difficult. It might be worth a try.

What you say and how you say it

What you say and how you say it are very important. For example, you'll find that "BUY ONE—GET ONE FREE" will always pull better than "SENSATIONAL HALF PRICE OFFER."

But what might really surprise you is that successful direct mail would often qualify for an "F" in an English composition class. If your sales letters are polished to perfection, there is a big chance they'll come off as compositions and that could be deadly. Direct mail writing is "selling"—not writing! You need sizzle, pizzazz, one-on-one salesmanship or you won't get the readership you deserve— or the great response you want.

This is not English Composition 101

What separates direct mail writing from English composition?

First and foremost, purpose. A composition, expository theme, and other "literary" writing is primarily written to entertain or educate. Direct mail has one purpose and one purpose only—TO SELL—it's your salesman.

There's an old story about a company president who discovered that the last direct mailing his firm sent out had brought in a landslide

> **Direct mail has one purpose and one purpose only— TO SELL.**

response. He was overjoyed. So he started investigating. He had the sales manager bring in a copy of the landslide-producing sales letter.

Red faced, the sales manager handed the letter to the president with this apology, *"Chief, I'm embarrassed about this letter. It got out by mistake. What happened was that one of our salesmen begged me to let him write a letter to take the place of the one we had been using. Frankly, I didn't check it out before it went to press."*

"What's the problem?" asked the Chief. *"Well—just look! Misspelled words, poor sentence structure, typos, pitiful grammar. It's a disgrace!"*

One look at the letter confirmed everything the sales manager had said. The president just smiled and said, *"Oh, well. Everybody will get a memo from me this afternoon about this letter."*

The sales manager, head hanging, skulked out of the office not doubting that his job was doomed.

That afternoon everyone got a memo from the president. It said, *"I ain't never seen nothin so bad in my hole life, that there letter you rit was horbal and I'm downright boled over by this here thing. The only thing what I ask is that the dum guy who rit it shud write all our sales letters and in his spare time help to figger out what to do with all the cash weer makin off'n it."*

Whatever works

True? Probably not, but it does emphasize a fundamental: *Use whatever works.* You're not shooting for an "A" in composition—you're shooting for the best response possible. You are selling, not writing. That is not to say that you shouldn't use proper grammar and correct spelling. I'm certainly not advocating careless writing.

Conversational tone

What I am advocating is a style that has been one of the overriding principles of direct mail advertising since the earliest days of the form: Write in the style in which you you speak. Of course, that doesn't mean in fits and starts with all the *"uh"s, "er"s* and *"you knows."* THAT would be disconcerting and hardly easy-to-read.

When I say use a conversational tone I'm talking about using an informal conversational tone, a personal me-to-you style.

This style has been called edited conversation. Use the conversational words you ordinarily use. Then go back and jettison the redundancies, the unclear expressions, the dull, the bland, the long rambling sentences. You may find that you have to articulate in words things that you ordinarily communicate with shrugs, gestures, and raised eyebrows. The idea is to get your meaning across in a comfortable, natural style.

Ann Landers is one of the most widely read columnists in the country. Why is she so popular?

"I was taught to write just as I talk," says Ann. *"Some people like it."*

People enjoy reading clear, simple, easy-to-understand writing. And the simplest, clearest style is to write just as you talk. The writing experts call this "conversational tone."

"Conversational tone is especially important in advertising, where

> **The idea is to get your meaning across in a comfortable, natural style.**

the printed page is an economical substitute for a salesperson."
—Robert Bly

Give them benefits

Okay, that's how you say it, but what do you say? Be sure to focus on benefits; tell your customer what your product will do for them.

Know your prospective customers—those to whom your product or service should appeal? Know what their self-interests are—and how your merchandise will satisfy their needs and desires. Address your ads to these people. Focus on their needs. People don't buy things, they don't buy features—they buy rewards, benefits.

A grass seed seller I know once commented, *"People couldn't care less about my grass seed. All they care about is their lawns."*

So, talk about their lawns. Use only the facts; emphasize but don't exaggerate. Overstating will turn off the reader. Visualizing your customer and how your product will benefit or enhance his or her life will help you write convincing ad copy.

If your promotion includes a free gift and/or a guarantee, be sure to emphasize those benefits.

Remember, your English teacher is not grading your sales letter. It'll be graded on how it pulls.

Experiment, experiment, experiment. Never stop experimenting with your ad copy. Keep polishing and refining to get it just right. Try to get everything just right. How will you know when it is just right? When it clicks. When it works and you're pulling in

> *Never stop experimenting with your ad copy. Keep polishing and refining to get it just right.*

responses. When it produces handsome financial returns.

Study what others are doing

Develop an awareness of advertising copy. Study ads. Rate them and articulate your reasons for the rating you give them. Watch for ads that are repeated over a length of time. If the same ad is repeated regularly, you can assume it's a winner. Spend some time with these ads and try to determine what it is that makes them winners. Test these methods in your own ads.

"One of the biggest reasons why a person doesn't buy a particular item or service is simply that he doesn't know he needs it. So it's your job to show him he's been pining for your product for many a moon—but didn't even know it!"—Luther Brock, Ph.D.

Give them basics

Don't assume too much about your prospective customers. They may not be familiar with your product. Give them the basics. Be careful in choosing your language; don't use too much jargon or industry talk. Conversational language and familiar, colloquial expressions are more easily understood, although much of the "sloppiness" of everyday language, as well as the plodding, the *dull-as-dishwater* words and phrases, should be eliminated. When you do use technical words or jargon, be sure to explain its meaning at that point. Use examples that your readers can identify with. Educate your reader—give him enough background information so he can read and understand your letter with ease.

Educate your prospective customer

The beauty of educating in a sales letter is that you'll have a receptive audience if you go at it in the right way. Your prospective customer want to be educated, he wants to learn; he wants to be with-it, up-to-the minute, an insider. So when you take the time to educate him, you're also grabbing his attention. But don't get tricky or cute or clever to the point where your offer is difficult to understand. Try to be simple, direct, and clear. Be specific and beware of multiple concepts that may confuse your reader.

Color and design

What about color and design? Well, color and design do have an impact. But no matter how fantastic they are, color and design have little to do with getting a great response *per se*. But like a display window, they do get your reader involved—they contribute to getting your mail read.

If I had to pick from an overly-art-directed mailing and a Plain Jane one, I'd go with Jane every time… because art can actually get in the way of comfortable reading.

For example, you have a "hot" deal so you print your letter on red paper to emphasize the "heat." Trouble is, black print is extremely difficult to read on a red background. Your reader is apt to say, *"Heck, I can't read this thing."* He'll toss it like a hot potato.

And then there are those sales letters with a dandy picture that seems to be stamped right over the writing. Some are very interesting—the artwork, I mean. I don't know about the message; sometimes it's to difficult to decipher.

If I had to pick from an overly-art-directed mailing and a Plain Jane one, I'd go with Jane every time.

The old standby white letter

You'll find the old standby white letter can't be beat. Oh, sure now and then a pale ivory or something is appropriate. But on the whole, you're better off with a letter that looks like a letter—black print on white paper.

Colored print?

Since the dark ages of direct mail, companies have been testing all sorts of ink colors. To date there is no reliable evidence that one color outpulls another.

Common sense says, of course, to not use red ink to sign your letter. It's unbusinesslike. And you don't want to convey the impression that you're "in the red."

Handwritten notes in the margins, freehand underscoring, signatures seem to come alive in blue or brown ink.

Brochures and folders

When it comes to brochures and folders, you can let loose—at least a little. Of course, a lot depends on your audience. For instance, you're better off staying with subdued colors when writing to upscale businesspersons. On the other hand, when writing to the masses go with colorful. It's a good contrast—emphasis.

The contrast sets the business letter apart from the inserts. Your reader will know right off the bat which is which. Fancy typefaces, such as script or swash styles, should be used sparingly. You want your entire mailing to be easy to read.

You want your entire mailing to be easy to read

Order forms

You never know what your prospect is going to look at first after opening your envelope. It could be your sales letter, your various enclosures, or your order form. Yet many order forms are tucked away in the recesses of the mailing! It's as if they were hiding out! Every part of your mailing should sizzle with salesmanship—including the order form. Think of it as part of your sales effort. So much can be done with it! It, too, should grab your reader's interest. It should make your reader want to fill it out. If your reader doesn't understand your offer just from reading your order form—there goes many a sale. It may be the only thing the prospect reads—so the message on the form should be a succinct encapsulation of your offer. Identify your product, the selling price, shipping information, guarantee and method of payment.

It's a good idea to have a stub for older recipients to keep. It could be headed "**Keep this stub for your records.**" Leave blanks for them to document the date ordered, product purchased, and so on.

Why for older people? There seems to be a correlation between age and trust. Anyway, a little stub perforated for easy detachment increases orders.

Be sure your order form is a separate enclosure, not just part of the sales letter. I know the bottom of the last page of the sales letter is a convenient place to put the order form and many people do—but don't. A separate form always pulls better. It looks more official.

Contrast the form with the personal look of the letter. Use borders and have it typeset.

Make your order form clear and easy to fill out.

Use pastel-colored paper for your order form. If you are mailing to strictly upscale prospects, a dignified black on white form may be ideal, but not for most mailings.

Try pastel colors, but not grays and tans—too dead looking. Or use white paper with colored borders. Make it stand out. You want your prospect to look at your order form.

Now let's talk about the most important part of your order form, the heading. Perhaps the worst possible heading you could employ for the order form is ORDER FORM.

Try to come up with a topic heading that pushes a benefit:

- •EXPRESS ORDER FORM

- •FREE-TRIAL ORDER FORM

- •LIMITED-TIME SPECIAL OFFER

Or make an interesting statement from the prospects point of view:

- •"YES, I WANT TO LOSE WEIGHT FAST!"

- •"I CAN'T WAIT FOR YOUR WIDGET TO ARRIVE!"

You get the picture. Ordinarily I would go with the topic heading. But as long as you are pushing benefits, your reader will read; just don't start pushing cleverness. Cleverness for the sake of cleverness is disastrous in direct mail—including the order form.

The mailing envelope

The mailing envelope, on the other hand, may be a different story. One fellow I know who sells a financial newsletter swears that yellow envelopes pull better. I sure won't try to dissuade him from using them.

Experiment

Find an envelope design that sparks people's interest. You may have the best sales letter in the world, but it won't do you a bit of good if your envelope doesn't get opened.

Avoid anything that gives the impression of "junk mail." Unless you're running a sweepstakes—where you'd cover the entire envelope with "bells and whistles"—you should try to make your envelope look important and professional. Everyone opens mail that looks as if it might be business correspondence, an official government notice, or a letter from his attorney.

What kind of envelope?

Let's start with the material your envelope is made from. It should be either white (weave) or a kraft Manila. If you have a choice between 24 lb. and 28 lb., go with the 28 lb. It's sturdier and will arrive looking crisp and new and not all worn out. Kraft envelopes hark back to the days when legal documents came in Manila-colored envelopes. To many past-40 consumers they still connote importance.

What about the size?

The bigger it is, the better it usually pulls. Number 10 envelopes may end up all in one bunch, sometimes bound with a rubber band by the postal clerks. A 6 x 9 catalog envelope will stand out. Even better are the 9 x 12 catalog envelopes. These are frequently the first to be opened.

Avoid anything that gives the impression of "junk mail."

I prefer a white 9 x 12 catalog envelope with a border of green arrows all around it with "**FIRST CLASS**" printed in big, bold letters.

Postage

Envelopes with postage stamps may get you a 5-to-15% better response than metered mail. Stamped mail seems more personal. Your postage costs are the same either way.

When you mail Bulk Rate, you can use precancelled bulk rate stamps. These create the impression of "First Class." Compact, low-cost hand-held stamping machines and large expensive stamping machines are available. Check with your office supply store.

Cash envelopes

Set your price at even money ($20 instead of $19.95). When you include a cash envelope for those people who prefer sending cash, even money will be easier to enclose. You will be surprised at how many people send cash in the mail.

Selling dinner by direct mail. *DINNER?*

Okay, direct mail may be great used as a mailorder system, but what if you have a retail business? Well, let's use a restaurant as an example. Not much in a restaurant that can be sold by direct mail, right? *Wrong.* How about dinner? *Dinner?* By direct mail? You think I'm joking, don't you? But no, I'm not joking. I'll show you one way of doing it: First, you need the names and addresses of a select group. Shall we say all of the Norwegians in your trading area? Now, compose a letter offering something special, such as the one on the facing page:

Envelopes with postage stamps may get you a 5-to-15% better response than metered mail.

High Brow Restaurant

Dear _____,

You are receiving this letter because you're of Norwegian heritage. My name is Jane Doe. I own the *High Brow Restaurant* in Anytown. Next month we'll be serving free *Rommegrad* with any entrée ordered by a Norwegian. Stop in. Celebrate your heritage with us. Our *"Velcommen Mat"* will be out to greet you!

Sincerely,

Jane Doe
Owner, *High Brow Restaurant*
P.S. Let me tell you—I know some Norwegians and *Rommegrad* will bring them in. So will *Lutefisk*, but that may drive the others out...

You could choose any group that you want to target, such as real estate agents, physicians, nurses, whatever. You probably don't want to offer everyone *Rommegrad*, but how about free desert or free wine? Make the letter friendly and engaging.

Mystery

You might even put some mystery into your letter. Suggest there is a reason for offering something free to that particular group. Tell them that if they come in you will tell them the reason. Maybe you just bought a new home and are feeling expansive toward real estate agents this month. Next month, perhaps you'll remember the birth of your oldest child and feel partial to the medical profession.

You see, you can sell dinner by direct mail! Just about any business can use direct mail effectively. All you need is a creative idea and a sales letter.

Mailing lists for maximum response

But no matter how great your promotional ideas and sales letters are, you won't get the maximum response if you don't have the right mailing list. So how are you going to locate the names and addresses of all of the Norwegians?

Compiled lists

For one thing, there are all varieties of mailing lists out there. You may want to look into compiled lists. For instance, if you have a restaurant or other retail establishment, you need a list that deals with your trading area. If you want to do a mailing to everyone in your area, you need what is called a compiled residents list.

Maybe you want a compiled custom residents list. For specific areas, order by zipcode. Or you can order lists sorted by profession, by type of living quarters, by ethnic background, by just about any category you can dream up.

Buyers' lists

If your business isn't limited to your locality, maybe a regional list isn't what you need. For example, you have a dandy little boat gadget that you would like to market to boat owners. Then you'd want a buyers' list—a list of people who own boats.

Do you have a large expensive, "luxury" item that you feel will appeal to only higher-income people? In that case, some of the list companies have their list coded so that you can choose a listing by socioeconomic status—for instance, by income level, educational level, marital status, and several other categories.

These sorted lists sound great—just the thing you need. But, how are you going to find these sorted lists?

List sources

There are several sources for good, categorized lists. First, in any fairly large city, you will probably find sources under Mailing Lists and/or Mailing List Brokers in your *Yellow Pages*. If you don't find any list brokers in your directory, check at your library (consult the reference librarian) for the phone books for any major city.

Another excellent source is the *Standard Rate & Data List Book (SRDS Direct Mail Lists Rates and Data)*. Your library should have this book. It contains descriptions of thousands of mailing lists. If you can't get it at your library, call SRDS at 312•256•6067. I highly recommend your using this book. It'll give you hundreds of direct-mail ideas!

National list companies

A couple of national list companies that you may want to check out:

R.L. Polk & Company, 404•447•1280

Donnelly List Marketing, 212•265•5403

I highly recommend your using the SRDS. It'll give you hundreds of direct-mail ideas.

Lists for ideas

Mailing lists allow you to connect directly and personally with the people who are your prospective customers. The marketing possibilities with direct mail are virtually unlimited.

If you have ideas, the lists you need to market them are out there.

If you're fresh out of ideas, the lists out there can give you marketing ideas.

Direct mail can bring you amazing results!

Chapter 10

How to Make the *Yellow Pages* Pull for You

Riddle: When someone opens the *Yellow Pages,* what are two things you immediately know about that person?

Answer:

1. He wants to purchase something.

2. He isn't sure where he should buy it.

Okay. Poor riddle. But interesting answers, aren't they?

Riddle: Which establishment will he choose?

Answer:

The establishment with the advertisement that catches the eye and interest.

Okay. No more riddles, I promise.

Is *Yellow Pages* advertising a waste?

A question, though. What happens if none of the ads catches the eye and interest? The answer? The money you spent on *Yellow Pages* advertising is down the drain unless you are located close to the buyer.

Seems like a waste, doesn't it? I mean, look, the customer is halfway there—you don't have to convince him to buy, you need only to convince him to choose you.

You'll find lots of that kind of waste in the *Yellow Pages*. Don't take my word for it. Take a look for yourself. How many ads do you see that would convince you to go farther than necessary to buy what you want or need? Not many, I'm betting.

Do your ads stand out from the rest? Will it convince a prospective customer to go an extra mile—or more—to buy from you?

How can you change that?

How can you make the *Yellow Pages* pull for you? Thumb through the *Yellow Pages*. What stands out? Where does your eye stop? Notice that the size of an ad makes a difference. The larger ad pulls the eye, doesn't it?

Let's take a closer look at the ads.

I'll generalize here, noting that individual directories may offer more options for ads.

- **Line ad**—a listing, consisting of the business name, address, and telephone is the most basic. And, I might add, pretty ineffective. Spruced up with larger type they look a little better. But effective? Not likely.

- **In-column space ad**—a bit larger but set in-column. The business name is set in bold capital letters. The address and telephone number is placed at the bottom of the ad in lighter type. In between, is text listing hours, location, and perhaps specialties. This is an improvement but not much.

- **Trade ad**—also set in-column and alphabetically. This ad features a the business name at the top, a trademark or logo, a couple of

---

Do your ads stand out from the rest?

lines of text, and your listing at the bottom. The major improvements here are the additions of the logo and the business name listed both at the top and the bottom of the ad.

- **Display ad**—larger than the column ad, can include illustrations. It offers greater flexibility of layout; the business can put what it wants in it, within limits. This ad can employ impact headlines, illustrations, and custom borders. The display ad is positioned according to size and seniority. They are grouped according to size with the larger ads closer to the start of the heading. Within each size grouping the ads are arranged by purchase date. It is accompanied by an in-column alphabetical listing with a referral to the display ad.

What's effective?

As you've probably guessed, the most effective of these ads is the display ad. But placed with other display ads, what will set it apart?

Size will improve its effectiveness for two reasons. Size determines positioning and size is eye catching. But placed, as they are, among all other ads of the same dimensions, how do you out-pull them?

What else can be done?

Let's consider a couple of Gary Halbert's axioms:

NUMBER ONE

Research has demonstrated that people are FIVE times as likely to read editorial matter, than that which appears to be an ad.

NUMBER TWO

When a person looks in the *Yellow Pages,* he or she is searching for a solution.

> *"Research has demonstrated that people are FIVE times as likely to read editorial matter, than that which appears to be an ad."*

Let's, for example, look at the section for tanning salons. When a buyer opens the *Yellow Pages* to this section, what does the person want? Well, it's probably safe to assume this customer wants a nice, even tan, perhaps wants it quickly, and probably wants convenience.

But, why? The customer wants to look and feel more attractive. Aha! Now we're getting somewhere. The solution the buyer is looking for in the *Yellow Pages* is to improve his or her appearance.

Now, here we have this person, who is feeling like an ugly, white worm and who wants to feel like a warmly-tanned sex symbol, checking out the *Yellow Pages* for a firm that will promise a quick-and-easy transformation. Among all those lookalike ads, the white worm sees one that resembles an editorial message with a "news" headline such as one of the following:

YOU'LL BE BEAUTIFULLY TAN FAST!

NEW SCIENTIFIC METHOD

WORKS FASTER THAN FLORIDA SUNSHINE!

-or-

YOUR QUICK, GORGEOUS TAN

WILL MAKE YOUR FRIEND THINK

YOU SPENT THE WEEK IN FLORIDA!

READ ABOUT OUR NEW METHOD

-or-

FROM WHITE TO GORGEOUS FAST!

READ ABOUT OUR METHOD FOR

A BEAUTIFUL TAN PRACTICALLY OVERNIGHT

Of course, the headline must not make promises that you can't back up in the "editorial" copy beneath. The copy should inform, educate, and then give a compelling reason for the poor white worm to choose your establishment.

In addition, it must resemble a news story taken from a newspaper.

Your story might read something like this:

FROM WHITE TO GORGEOUS FAST!

READ ABOUT OUR METHOD FOR

THE FASTEST BEAUTIFUL TAN POSSIBLE!

Not all tanning salons are the same! Some know and use the *Quick Tan* secrets for a faster, deeper, more even tan. This method uses new and proven techniques to bring out the warm, golden hues hidden in your skin in the fastest, safest way known.

Your skin type is carefully analyzed to create a tanning program designed especially for you. Imagine, a custom program! Don't take chances with a program designed for the "average skin." Do what's best for your skin.

But that's not all! The *Quick Tan* people know that tanning bulbs have a limited effective life. They keep bulb time charts. You won't waste your time under ineffective bulbs. Your benefit? The fastest tan you can possibly achieve!

All of the associates at Electric Beach, Ltd. are trained in the *Quick Tan Method* to assure you a beautiful, safe tan faster than you thought possible.

Phone now for a free skin analysis.

Set the column in newspaper print and in two columns. Make it look like news, not an ad. Your "editorial" ad should offer:

- News
- A solution
- Something free, if possible

How large need your ad be to be effective?

Of course, it must be large enough to contain your "editorial." Also, a two-column width will distinguish it from the in-column ads. If there are large ads or numerous ads in your category, a large size will help your ad stand out. Go for the largest ad economically feasible.

Who should design your display ads?

Don't think that size alone is the measure of a good ad. And don't trust the magazine or newspaper staff to design your ad for you; they're in the business to sell ad space, not design effective, sales-producing ads. Although there are many exceptions, some of the most banal, money-wasting ads you see in magazines and news-papers are produced by in-house publication staffs. Your display ads

Don't trust the magazine or newspaper staff to design your ad for you ...

should be professionally designed, preferably by a good, independent designer or ad agency—and the designer should rely heavily upon your advice about your particular business and your targeted prospects. Attempting to shave your costs by designing an ad yourself or by relying upon the staff of the publication to do it is a prime example of the adage "penny wise and pound foolish." Shop around among a few good ad writer/designers or agencies.

Choose your headings with care

Ask yourself which headings a prospective customer would be likely to look under. If you feel that there is more than one heading that would be effective for you, go for it. You are allowed to place an ad under more than one heading.

Check your ads

You should get complimentary copies of all *Yellow Page* directories you advertise in. When you get the directory, check your ads. Make sure they are under the correct headings and the telephone numbers are correct and check your placement under the heading.

Also, check out the other ads under your headings. Now's the time to make note of any changes and improvements you'd like to see in the next directory.

Monitor for effectiveness

As with all your advertising, *Yellow Pages* advertising should be monitored for effectiveness. There are several ways you can monitor your ads' results. The most obvious is direct survey—asking your customers and charting the results. Ask all of your new prospects, including telephone callers and new walk-in customers.

... your ads should be professionally designed by a good designer or ad agency.

You could install a new number just for your *Yellow Pages* ads. This number cannot be used in any other ads if you are to get accurate survey results.

Remote Call Forwarding works well for monitoring ads containing that number. All you need do is check your telephone bill to get an accurate count of the calls generated by the ad.

If you have placed your ad under several headings or in several directories, your survey will tell you little about which ads have the best pull unless you key them. Some advertisers use phrases such as: *"A 10% discount for mentioning this ad."* Or use a fictitious name your customers should ask for: *"Ask for Blake."* Other advertisers put a number or letter in their ads and ask the caller to identify it.

Your first task is to design an effective ad.

Accurate surveys are important assuming your ad induces prospective customers to call your establishment. For good results from *Yellow Pages* advertising, your first and foremost task is to create an effective ad. The person looking in the *Yellow Pages* is a buyer looking for a place to make his purchase.

One more riddle

Remember the riddle? *"Which establishment will they choose?"* The answer was, *"The establishment with the advertisement that catches the eye and interest."*

I promised no more riddles, but I'm going to fudge and ask you one more: *"Will that establishment be yours?"*

Chapter 11

Alternative Marketing Strategies

The long-time leader of China, diminutive Deng Xiao Peng, was once asked about what is the best political system to get things done. He said, *"It doesn't matter what color the cat is as long as it catches the mouse."*

Deng's comment struck a chord with me in terms of marketing. Our goal is to sell our products or services and make money. Sometimes that means trying all kinds of different things—marketing things— to catch that elusive mouse made out of money. We shouldn't be afraid to try alternative methods to reach our end-goal.

To paraphrase the old Chinese leader: *"It doesn't matter what kind of marketing strategy you use, as long as that strategy achieves its goal: it makes you money."*

In this chapter, we are going to look at some very interesting alternatives to what we have discussed so far, including repackaging, joint venture and forced distribution, and perhaps even a few others. *Let's go!*

Alternative #1: Repackaging for brand-new markets

A friend asked me recently if he should try to come out with a new book annually to stay competitive in the market.

My advice is not to create something totally different from what you are now selling until you have pursued every means of marketing your existing product. The best strategy is to repackage your best-selling, proven products and market them to a brand-new audience.

One of my former newsletter subscribers sold thousands of books on his subject for less than $15. Then he offered the same basic information in weekend seminars costing $250 per person. The seminars were always sold out months in advance. Same product. Different approach. I call it repackaging.

Beyond the horizon

What does it take? Imagination. You have to look through the binoculars of imagination beyond the horizon of the market you are now serving. If one market will buy your product in one package, others will also pay for it if you package in the way they prefer.

The embroidery hoop

Take the embroidery hoop. Years ago women did a lot of time-consuming fancy sewing. Embroidery hoops sold. Then along came the age of women working at jobs outside the home. Suddenly very few women have the time or inclination for fancy sewing, but a lot of them have a need for a quicker creative outlet. The embroidery hoop has become central to many creative projects that aren't as time-consuming as fancy sewing—not as a tool but as an element of the finished product. The embroidery hoop is still an embroidery

Look through the binoculars of imagination beyond the horizon of the market you are now serving.

hoop but it is perceived differently. If it hadn't acquired a new image, the hoop would certainly not sell as it does today.

It's all in how you perceive things

For instance, if you see yourself as a book publisher, that's what you'll be. But if you see yourself as a complete information source, you may envision a panorama of market segments in which to sell your product or service.

You'll see that reaching your goal in one market segment is not necessarily an indication that you must look for a new product or service to promote. It could be that it's time to begin reaching for new goals in another segment of the market with the same product.

It was Thomas Watson of IBM who said, *"Whenever an individual or a business decides that success has been attained, progress stops."*

Do you feel you've reached your goal with a certain product and are ready to move on to another product? Before you move on, try marketing your already-tested-and-proven product to a new market.

Let me tell you about another of my former newsletter readers. He sold millions of dollars worth of his $10 book. Then he put the same information on cassette tape and sold it for $25! People pay gladly for a more convenient form of a product.

Premium purchase inducements

Build bonuses into your package. A low-cost bonus with a high perceived value can do wonders for your sales. Also you could look for opportunities to package your product to offer to other companies for use as bonuses or premiums.

Complementary repackaging

Let's say you have been marketing a great software program for organizing customer lists. It's a contacts manager, and it's a convenient method for compiling and sorting names, addresses, and phone numbers of customers. But you're floundering. You can't quite seem to whip up enough enthusiasm to generate the sales you feel that this product warrants.

Now let's say you run across a clever little label-making program. This computer program is also floundering in the marketplace. What if you were to repackage your contacts manager on a complementary plan with the label-printing program; on the other hand, you might combine the programs into an all-in-one contacts manager/label printing program? You both might even join forces and offer the pair of programs (or combined program) at a discounted price to the manufacturer of a popular label-printing device. Both (or all three) products will enjoy greater appeal. The package is a great deal and convenience for your customers.

Repackaging your advertising

You can also repackage your advertising. Presenting your message in a different manner can make a real difference. Try different combinations—always try to find something that will outperform what you are currently doing.

Small changes can make a big difference

It's like giftwrapping. Pretty paper does the job satisfactorily, but a small thing such as adding a bow makes it special.

Consider this:

"We're now offering 25% off our gadget!"

"Save $50 when you buy from us!"

"Put $50 back in your pocket!"

"Put $50 into your savings account!"

All of these headlines say the same thing in different packaging. Do you think one may be more effective than the others?

"It is not uncommon for a change in headlines to multiply returns from five to ten times over."—Claude Hopkins

If one ad pulls $5000 and another $25,000, use the most effective one? Your ad will cost the same whichever headline you run.

Just to illustrate that small things make a big difference, let me tell you about a book that was advertised under two different titles. The titles weren't much different—*"Art of Kissing"* and *"Art of Courtship."* Both titles were run in national newspapers. Exposure was equal. One sold 60,500 copies in a year; the other sold 17,500 copies during the same time period. The best selling title? *"Art of Kissing."* Why? Because, according to Dr. George W. Crane, *"Customers buy the specific versus the general. You don't say 'I'll take food' when a waitress asks you for your order in a restaurant."*

Do you need to repackage your advertising into a more specific statement of customer benefits? Will a small change make your ad more specific and more effective?

Small changes without rewriting

Repackage your ad—and increase its response—without rewriting it. How? Change the headline to a bold, sans serif style; change the body copy (text) from a sans serif typestyle to serif. (Serif type, in case you're unfamiliar with the term, has the "little feet" under most characters. Sans serif is plain, without "feet." The text you're reading now is a routine example of a serif typestyle. [Sans serif type, on the other hand, is used in this sentence.] Tests show that, generally speaking, serif type is often more "reader-friendly" in text or body copy; conversely, a bold sans serif works well for headlines. Also, try using contrast. Make that headline "reversed," in other words, white, bold print against a solid-color or black background. Use catchy words and phrases instead of dull, pedestrian prose; typical examples are *"All-New!," "New & Improved," "Doctor-Recommended," "Discover,"* and others. Folks like things that are *"new & improved"*; they like to *"discover"* things. Stay away from *"incredible."* It's the most over-used adjective in advertising. Almost everything under the sun is ballyhooed as *"incredible."* Even if your product or service is indeed *incredible*, try *"phenomenal"* or *"unbelievable"* or *"sensational"* or *"awesome"* or *"exceptional"* or *"peerless"* or *"without competition."* As you can see, if you're going to write (or help write) your own ad copy, purchasing a good thesaurus will quickly prove to be a worthy investment.

Such little things, yet overlooking them can cost you thousands of dollars. Goes to demonstrate that details are important.

Folks like things that are "new & improved"; they like to "discover" things...

Not just printed messages

But your message needn't be in printed form. You can repackage your personal sales messages, too. If your salespeople in the field present their message in a new package and produce three times as many sales, what's it worth to you?

Can changing their sales presentation increase each average sale? Can it increase the ratio of active buyers per presentation? Keeping a salesperson in the field costs roughly the same whether he or she sells $30,000 or $90,000 a month, whether he converts 5% or 50% of his leads.

Similarly, perhaps repackaging a promotion without a significant increase in costs will pull five times the sales.

Demand results

Experiment. Repackage. Challenge your marketing techniques. Demand results from every marketing dollar you spend—for advertising, promotional campaigns, salespeople and training.

Alternative #2: Complementary (Joint Venture) Marketing

A lot of companies have products or services which are non-competitive, or, better yet, complementary—and not at all competitive. But they may be targeting overlapping market segments. In fact, they may be working the very same customer base. Each firm would have customers that are logical prospects for the other. Complementary marketing could be beneficial to both companies.

Experiment. Repackage. Challenge your marketing techniques. Demand results from every marketing dollar you spend.

For example, let's say your company has a product that is non-competitive or complementary with a product another company is promoting in your market segment. You are both targeting upscale, affluent prospects in a three-state area. Perhaps the other company has been in business for several years. It has built up a list of the upscale people you are targeting in the same geographical area. That company has expended a lot of time, energy and money massaging and developing that particular market population and location.

You could spend the same amount of time and money to do the same—or you could approach the company and make an arrangement with them.

You could offer them a percentage of the sales that you generate from the list. With this deal, the other company gets to recoup some of the expenses they incurred in developing the list. And you get to reap full advantage of their marketing efforts.

On the other hand, maybe the situation is reversed. Perhaps you have been in business for several years and have compiled a list that would be perfect for another company.

Approach them and offer them the opportunity to benefit from your years of marketing efforts for a percentage of the sales generated. With this deal, you can further benefit from the list that you compiled while the other company gets to take advantage of your marketing experience. Either way, it's a win-win.

Or, perhaps you're using a direct mail campaign and so is the other company. You've rented a mailing list; the other company is renting the same list. Each company has incurred printing expenses. Your company and the other company have matching postage expenses.

It's easy to see how entering into a joint campaign would reduce the costs of the advertising for both you and the other company. The mailing lists and the postage would cost about the same for two companies as they do for one. In a joint mailing, each would end up with about one-half of the mailing expense.

If your products are truly compatible, each company may experience an increase in sales generated by offering the consumer the convenience of a joint offer.

You've no doubt seen automatic clothes washers that include a brand of laundry detergent with their delivery. In effect, the washer company is endorsing that brand of detergent—and vice versa. These are entirely complementary products that are not competitive.

Do you and another company have products that go together like salt and pepper, sugar and cinnamon, or bacon and eggs?

If the products were packaged together, would they enhance one another? Is it possible that the package deal would have a perceived value greater than each single product now enjoys? Would the package be more attractive to the consumer or more likely to catch the consumer's attention?

If the two products are of equal value, working out a deal would be easy—just split the expenses and the revenues. If the products are of unequal value, an arrangement can still be arrived at by prorating everything. But what if the products are of a grossly inequitable value? What if you are the "detergent" and the other company is the "clothes washer," so to speak.

In this case, perhaps you'll provide your product for the package deal at little or no charge. The cost of providing the product is your payment for the endorsement, the advertising, and the opportunity to be the first brand used by the consumer in the new washer.

Your detergent is guaranteed to go out to someone who is washing clothes; someone who may be concerned about using the "right" detergent in a new washer. The thing to evaluate here is how likely the consumer is to stay with the brand recommended and provided by the manufacturer of the new machine.

A lot of companies have totally compatible, non-competitive products that would work well in joint venture packaging and marketing. It's just that most have never thought of what complementary marketing could do for them.

Alternative #3: Forced Distribution

Forced distribution is exactly what it sounds like. You walk up to your customer, put a gun to his head and say *"Buy this or I pull the trigger!!"* Just kidding. Actually forced distribution of your wares or services, is forcing them upon the marketplace in a different way. Ironically, "forcing distribution" is the process of inducing consumers to demand that your product be made available to them.

How can distribution be forced?

Remember my client whose offer was a reproduction of a wedding certificate dating from the 1800s? He mailed out a few news releases and got a great response. He invested some of the income into mailing out more releases. Then large mail-order catalog houses saw his stories, and he began getting calls from them. They were interested in adding his product to their catalogs!

Newspaper publicity can mushroom fast. If your story is picked up by the wire services (such as AP or UPI) or a syndicated column, it can suddenly appear in newspapers from coast to coast.

Once you get the publicity and your merchandise is selling well, mail-order catalogs will want to display it. Talk about distribution!

Even if it doesn't do well by their standards, big companies that send out millions of catalogs need thousands of units of your product to cover the orders they do receive.

Forcing distribution with news articles

Similarly, you can introduce your product to independent retail outlets across the nation with news articles.

I helped one of my clients force distribution of his sports items to retail outlets by using news articles announcing that it was available at sporting goods stores. (It was available—in about three.)

People read the news stories and mobbed the stores. Most, of course, didn't have it in stock. Consumer demand created distribution! The stores were forced to order the product—and immediately—or miss out on all those sales. Hence the expression, forced distribution. My client was happy to help them out. He simply wholesaled stock to the stores in lots of 144 units each. The stores did the selling.

Create consumer demand. Distribution will follow!

Force distribution through "couponing." Have you wondered at the proliferation of coupons? Open a Sunday newspaper or look in a few magazines. You'll find reams of coupons.

In fact, coupons literally fall out of the paper into your lap, and many magazines seem to have coupons on every other page. And they're not nickel-and-dime coupons, either. Many are worth a lot. What's going on?

"Couponing" is an effective method of forcing distribution. Blitz your area with coupons. Make the offer appealing. What happens?

Dozens of customers descend on the stores, coupon in hand, demanding merchandise that many of the stores don't have in stock. The merchant doesn't want to disappoint regular customers and certainly doesn't want to send them to the competition.

Would you want to admit that the competition is better-stocked or more up-to-date than your store is? No, of course not. More likely, you'd promise to have it in stock as soon as possible. You might even say you have it on order. Then you'd place an order on the double. Forced distribution.

Forcing distribution through warehouses

It's also possible to force distribution into retail chain stores through warehouses, though it's not quite as simple as using the publicity and advertising route.

Have you noticed that many retail chains run approximately the same ad for all of their stores? The reason? Often the ads are set up

---

"Couponing" is an effective method of forcing distribution. Blitz your area with coupons.

and printed by the chain company's head office. The stores may be independently owned but they're locked into using the company's ad program through agreement.

The ad program may be a part of the franchise agreement, or it may simply be that the arrangement cuts the retailer's advertising costs considerably.

Why is it cheaper to run a company ad? One reason, of course, is the parent company or headquarters can probably cut a better deal with the printer based on the volume involved in printing ads for all of their stores. But there's another reason—the money the parent company receives for running specific products in the ads. Manufacturers, brokers and distributors pay (either in cash or in deep discounts) to get their products into the ads. Why? Their product is guaranteed to be displayed in the ads of dozens of independent retailers. And they know all of those retailers will be forced to order enough of their product to cover anticipated sales.

When the sale is over many of the retailers will have some left-over unsold stock. What will they do with it? Probably give it a spot on their shelves where, it is hoped, it will become a regularly stocked item. Forced distribution.

Dealing with large chain companies requires dealing in person with company buyers, and the initial distribution could be quite costly. If you have the resources to pull it off, it's a way to force your product into the retail markets.

Let's say you have a new food product called *Barfy Snak* that costs you $0.50 to produce and package. You're selling to independent retailers for $1.50 and suggesting a retail of $2.25.

You're doing okay, but you would like to increase your outlets for the product. You decide you could take a smaller markup if you could increase your volume and decrease your delivery costs. So you approach a chain company. To put it in their ad, they make demands. You will realize only 45¢ per unit—a loss of 5¢ on each. This initial order will cost you BIG.

If you accept this deal, you will be gambling that future orders will be sufficient to cover this loss and make you a profit. How many of their stores will continue to carry your product after the sale? Their customers' introduction to your product will be at a sale price. What will this do to your price image? Will their customers be willing to purchase it later at regular price?

With an item that people will possibly buy repeatedly and regularly, this method of forced distribution may be worth the risks involved.

If, however, your product is not likely to be purchased frequently and repeatedly, you may saturate the market at a loss and sell yourself out of prospective customers. In this case, forced distribution at a loss is not such a good idea. You'll want to cut a deal at a decent profit for you on the initial order.

Personally, I prefer to force distribution by the news article route. It's an easier, more profitable, and certainly less risky way to force distribution.

Alternative #4: Insert Programs

This is all about hitching a ride on some else's information and distribution efforts. Many of you have probably seen brochures and inserts in your monthly electric bill, or in your box of new check blanks. These are marketing efforts by people who have made agreements with other people who are mailing out something anyway. You say to those people: *"Since you're already sending that mailer to your 75,000 customers, why not let us share some of the mailing cost by including or advertisement within your envelope? Our item won't interfere with your business, and may even enhance it by giving people something that they want."*

If the distributor of origin agrees, you have insert program.

It's a matter of sharing. With insert programs you can enlarge your customer base at a modest cost. It's similar to carpooling. If four people are going to the same place at the same time, they can get there for less cost (and less stress and hassle) by pooling. Insert programs are numerous and varied but they all have one thing in common: they convey a sales or advertising message that is inserted for delivery in someone else's carrier. The obvious benefit to you is lower distribution cost because the cost is shared.

Who makes the rules?

The marketers who provide and/or distribute the carriers own the programs. Your advertising and that of other participants just takes advantage of the delivery.

The rules are determined by the program owners. Reasonable enough. Sometimes many insert advertisers are included in a single

With insert programs you can enlarge your customer base at a modest cost.

vehicle, sometimes only one. Usually the programs are planned to avoid competition with the owner and with the other insert advertisers included a particular package.

A variety of carriers

As I said, there is a variety of carriers that deliver inserts. Advertising can be inserted in:

- A monthly utility bill
- A monthly credit card bill
- A monthly bank statement
- Any similar monthly mailing
- A magazine blow-in card
- A direct-carrier mailing, called a co-op mailing
- A co-op type mailing inserted in a newspaper
- A mailorder delivery
- A photo finishing envelope
- Any product or service delivery
- A paperback book, as a bound-in card
- Another marketer's catalog
- Any retail product box or carton

The list can go on and on. Insert programs can be developed for nearly any type of delivery.

Choosing the right insert program

Although choosing the right insert program is as important as choosing a mailing list, it is more difficult. Look for a program that is managed well. Keep demographics and psychographics in mind—

where the package is going and to whom.

If you are planning to hitch a ride with a merchandise delivery carrier, the delivery could affect the effectiveness of your campaign. Depending on your offer, the merchandise can heighten or depress the response.

Be sure to consider all aspects of the mailing program before you commit yourself.

Make sure you meet the deadlines

When you do commit to a program, make sure you know the deadlines—and make sure your printer and all other responsible parties know, too. Allow enough leeway in timing to cover any delay in shipping. The carrier will go without your insert, if it isn't there on time. As with any public transportation, they won't wait for you.

Forms of inserts

What form should your insert take? The variety is limited only by your imagination, although different programs have different physical limitations. You could use a reply card, flyer, folder, wallet, pamphlet, envelope, you name it. Usually, the maximum size allowed is your best bet. You don't want your insert to be a midget among giants. It could get lost or overlooked.

Testing

As with all advertising, your insert advertising must be tested. When first testing, use copy and design that you already know works in direct mail so you are testing the effectiveness of the program and not the copy or offer. In marketing parlance you are isolating the number of variables to just the program itself. Test several markets at one time to obtain comparison figures. Put at least 10,000 inserts into each program to ensure statistically-reliable measurements.

Be patient

For evaluation of returns, you'll have to be patient. Insert programs, especially those accompanying retail merchandise, are distributed more slowly than other distribution methods so returns come in more slowly. Allow plenty of time before evaluating the program.

Key your inserts

Testing will be fruitless if you have no way of knowing which ads your customers are responding to. Be sure to key your inserts so you know which mailings are pulling.

Retesting and analyzing

If you get a favorable response from a certain program, retest immediately. Keep a step ahead of a competitor who may be waiting to profit from your testing. On the other hand, don't drop your marginal programs without analyzing them. Can you renegotiate your cost of participating in the program or economize on your printing? Can you save enough on these costs to change marginal to profitable? You could revamp your insert or offer and test again.

The response rate from an insert program will be lower than from direct mail. Remember, though, that your insert distribution costs are only a fraction of direct mail costs. Instead of judging your test returns on raw response, use a cost-per-return basis. Measure your success not by response but by profit.

More than one way to skin a cat

Look closely at your method of doing business. There is more than one method of profiting from insert programs. Does your business lend itself to operating an insert program? If you do regular mailings or shipping merchandising packages, you have the potential of serving as a carrier for inserts for other companies.

There's More

In this chapter we've looked at just a few alternative marketing methods. Actually, writing an entire book on the subject may not be a bad idea. There's always a new way to try things, a new angle, a new method. Some unique marketing methods are out there waiting to be created—perhaps by you!

If you do become the first to find a new method of reaching customers and making sales, the value of your find could translate to a big boost in your firm's bottom line. So get out there, use your head and see what you can come up with!

Chapter 12

Two Big Items:
Cash Flow and Leverage

Have you ever read Claude Hopkins' excellent book *Scientific Advertising*? It is a *must read!* In fact, I recommend that you read and reread it at least a half-dozen times during the next year. You will learn more about testing, selling and money-making methods that you could learn on your own in two lifetimes!

Claude also wrote a book called *My Life in Advertising*; both books are combined into one volume and are available from:

NTC Publishing Group

4255 West Touhy Avenue

Lincolnwood, IL 60646

phone 708•679•5500

"Scientific advertising" is the process of carefully testing the market and measuring your results, taking care to continually adjust your advertising variables (where you advertise, what size ads, what style ads, which ad copy works best, *et al.*) until your advertising program does its intended job of generating a nice profit.

Your success depends on pleasing people. By employing an inexpensive test, you can learn if you please them or not. You can guide your endeavors accordingly. That is your best way to advertising success.

"Perhaps one time in fifty a guess may be right. But fifty times in fifty, an actual test tells you what to do and what to avoid." —Claude Hopkins

Scientific advertising isn't in the "beauty contest" business—it's designed to be effective but not necessarily glamorous. It may not win artistic awards. Rather, it is meant to work for you as your salesman-in-print or salesmanship multiplied.

Salesmanship-in-print is precisely the same as salesmanship-in-person.

Ad copy writers may forget that they are salesman and attempt to be performers; instead of sales, they seek applause. Beware of this tendency.

"To apply scientific advertising, one must recognize that ads are salesmen. One must compare them, one-by-one, on a salesman's basis and hold them responsible for cost and result."—Claude Hopkins

You work out a sales talk, write it down, and put it in front of people's eyes through the media. And what if it doesn't work? Hey, no problem! You do small, inexpensive tests until the results tell you exactly what you need to do to get the money rolling in.

"Almost any question can be answered cheaply, quickly, and finally by a test campaign. And that's the way to answer them—not by arguments around the table."—Claude Hopkins

> **Ad copy writers may forget that they are salesmen and try to be performers; beware of this tendency.**

Then you take that proven sales talk and make that 'perfected sales call' to thousands of prospects through the mail or media. You are duplicating your efforts—that's salesmanship multiplied!

"Superlative claims do not count. To say that something is "the best in the world" makes no impression whatever. The reader naturally minimizes whatever else we say. Give actual figures, state definite facts."—Claude Hopkins

Using that tested "perfected sales talk" is the heart of scientific advertising. That's why it's scientific. Until you test, it's just a guess. When you do what the market has told you to do and what your tests prove really work, there is little worry or risk in expanding your sales as fast as you can.

Leverage your ads. Find the combination that produces the maximum sales and profits. The cost is important, of course, but only in relation to the pull. An expensive ad that produces big profits is an excellent buy; a cheap ad that makes nothing happen is a loser no matter how you judge it. Gauge the success of your marketing by the response. Don't forget to look at the cost per response.

For example, let's say you are choosing between marketing campaigns for your $20 product. **Campaign A** will cost you $1,000 and **Campaign B** will cost $2,000. Which will you spring for? If you're looking at cost only, you'll choose **Campaign A**.

Cost in itself, however, is meaningless. For instance, let's say the campaigns pulled 50,000 and 6,000,000 responses respectively. Then the cost per response is $.02 for **Campaign A** and $.0003 for

An expensive ad that produces big profits is an excellent buy; a cheap ad that makes nothing happen is a loser no matter how you judge it.

Campaign B. Obviously you're getting a better return on your marketing investment with the second campaign.

Testing provides you with the information you need to choose the campaign that gives you the most leverage for your dollar, the one that provides you the maximum sales and profit.

Isn't that what you really want? To make a lot more money while doing a lot less work, and investing as little as possible for maximum return?

CASH FLOW + LEVERAGE = FINANCIAL FREEDOM

Customers bring in the sales and cash flow. But what brings you customers? Marketing. Not just haphazard marketing—planned marketing. Your marketing must follow a plan.

Cash flow, leverage, and financial freedom—all this begins with a sound marketing plan, and that brings us right back to where we started.

Afterword

What's It All About, Anyway?

ENJOY YOURSELF!

THIS IS NOT A DRESS REHEARSAL.

THIS IS YOUR LIFE!

–From a sign above the desk of my friend Ted Thomas–

Years from now, when you are on your deathbed, and you look back on you life, what do you want to remember the most about your life, and feel the best about?

Are you going to say to yourself with your last breath: *"Gee, I wish I had spent more time at the office."* Or, *"If only I could have pulled another 2 percent on my Widget-A campaign, my life would have had more meaning ..."* I don't think so. Yes, you want to make a lot of money, do the best job you can, but most of all, you want to have a decent, happy, challenging, worthwhile life. If marketing of any sort is a part of that life, then the marketing itself must somehow achieve those things for you: it must make you happy, it must challenge you and give your life *real* meaning and *real* fulfillment.

That means marketing for love—and perhaps this is the most important bit of advice yet offered in these pages. The fact is, HOW you market can make or break your business. In my mind, there's only one way to market... with *love*.

You need to enjoy it—LOVE IT—DO IT WITH ENTHUSIASM!

If you're in it just for the money, your enthusiasm will flag. Oh, sure, you'll be enthusiastic some of the time, but you won't be able to keep it up 100% of the time.

And if you're not enthusiastic about it, how are you going to whip up enthusiasm in your prospective customers? Can you really expect them to get enthusiastic and run right out and buy a product that you're not excited about?

Many people's tombstones should read, *"Died at 30. Buried at 60."* —Nicholas Murray Butler

Stay alive! Sell something that you *love*, that you're excited about, that you enjoy working with, that you have a passion for! Something that commands your enthusiasm. Project that enthusiasm!

I guarantee you will make more money with a product or service you're excited about. And your life will be more enjoyable, as well.

Life is to be enjoyed, savored, lived with a passion. If you love your line of work, your work will become a game. A fun game with big rewards. Enthusiasm works almost like magic!

It's been convincingly documented in a research study done by Srully Blotnick, Ph.D. Blotnick is a best-selling financial writer who headed a group of researchers who tracked 1500 people over a period of 20 years.

They divided the people into two groups—**Group 1**, those who had chosen their careers for the money and **Group 2**, those who had chosen their careers for the love of the field.

> **Stay alive! Sell something that you love, that you're excited about, that you enjoy working with, that you have a passion for!**

Group 1, 83% of the total, wanted to make lots of money right now and planned to live the good life later.

Group 2, only 17% of the total, wanted to make money, too, but wanted to enjoy life right away. They wanted to live their dream; they were in love with their chosen field of endeavor.

The results of the project after 20 years are astonishing.

Of the 1500, 101 people had become millionaires. Of the 101, fully 100 were from **Group 2**. Over 99% of the millionaires were spawned by less than 17% of the participants! They followed their dreams and pursued what they loved and found financial success and fulfillment.

"The evidence points overwhelmingly to the fact that work you enjoy is far more likely to make you rich..."—Srully Blotnick, Ph.D.

But what if you're stuck with a product you're not stuck on?

That is to say, your product's okay, but it just doesn't light your fire. What then?

If you can't fall in love with your merchandise, fall in love with the process of marketing. Have a ball devising and implementing your marketing plan, your marketing strategy.

INC. magazine surveyed 665 chief executive officers and found that 88% feel that the success of their business is based upon an "ordinary idea"—an ordinary product, an ordinary service. But they SOLD that idea as if their livelihoods depended on it!

"The evidence points overwhelmingly to the fact that work you enjoy is far more likely to make you rich."

"We always hear most about the guy with the one big idea. But the fact is, these people followed a logical progression—and succeeded by taking an ordinary idea and pulling it off exceptionally well."
—George Gendron, Editor of INC.

Fall in love with the process of marketing. Make your marketing strategy interesting. Make it so interesting that it builds your enthusiasm.

To quote Bette Midler, *"You don't have to be beautiful—just very, very enthusiastic."*

Enthusiasm—that's the key! Become addicted to the fun and challenge of this "game." Don't do it just for the money. Do it for the fun and the challenge.

Find out what motivates your customers. Get to know what they are looking for—what convinces them to purchase your product.

Use your imagination. Try to predict the results of an unorthodox approach. Make it fun for you and for your customers.

Then almost any legitimate product or service can work for you!

Forget the dress rehearsal, this is your life. Enjoy it! Be enthusiastic! The rewards will follow.

Enthusiasm— that's the key! Don't do it just for the money. Do it for the fun and the challenge.

YOUR ACTION PLAN CHECKLIST

Get started right now.

Find a pen and some paper. Turn to the One-day Marketing Plan questions. Begin answering questions. Answer to the best of your ability without research. Skip those that you don't have the answers to. You can return to those later.

Answer the questions in each section. Don't worry about form at this point. You'll get to that later.

❏ Get started right now.

❏ Organize your answers into a marketing plan. It's easy. Just follow the examples shown in the chapter.

❏ Get started right now.

❏ Take control of your marketing—put your plan into action. Plan a refining-your-plan schedule.

❏ Get started right now.

❏ Refine your plan using the steps described in the *Refining Your Plan* section of Chapter 2. Check out later chapters for strategy ideas.

❏ Get started right now.

❏ I sincerely hope your plan brings you success. Remember to keep trying and testing until you have a winner, then keep testing. Have fun, be enthusiastic!

❏ Get started right now.

❏ Let me know about your success! I get just as excited as my clients do (sometimes more so) about their success. Share your success with me, so I can enjoy the good news along with you and congratulate you on a job well done.

If you enjoyed this book please let me know. I can't answer due to the volume of mail I receive, but I do sincerely appreciate your comments and enjoy hearing from you. I get picture postcards from all over the world with nice notes written by my customers and it makes my day.

❏ Get started right now.

❏ Get started right now.

❏ Get started right now.

❏ Get started right NOW!

❏ Be a success—*just DO it!*

Index

D

E

F

G

H

I

J

K

L

M

N

O

P

R

S

T

U

W

Y

The Business Bookshelf

These books have been carefully selected as the best on these subjects.
Your satisfaction is guaranteed or your money back.

Money Sources for Small Business

How You Can Find Private, State, Federal, and Corporate Financing 2nd Edition

By William Alarid. Many potential successful business owners simply don't have enough cash to get started. *Money Sources* shows how to get money from Federal, State, Venture Capital Clubs, Corporations, Computerized Matching Services, Small Business Investment Companies plus many other sources. Includes samples of loan applications.

ISBN 0-940673-73-8   224 pages   8½ x 11   paperbound
$19.95

Small Time Operator

How to Start Your Own Business, Keep Your Books, Pay Your Taxes, and Stay Out of Trouble

By Bernard Kamaroff, C.P.A. The most popular small business book in the U.S., it's used by over 250,000 businesses. Easy to read and use, *Small Time Operator* is particularly good for those without bookkeeping experience. Comes complete with a year's supply of ledgers and worksheets designed especially for small businesses, and contains invaluable information on permits, licenses, financing, loans, insurance, bank accounts, etc.

ISBN 0-917510-10-2   190 pages   8½ x 11   paperbound
$15.95

The International Instant Business Plan

Twelve Quick and Easy Steps to a Successful Business

By Gustav Berle, Ph.D., and Paul Kirschner for international entrepreneurs. Learn the secrets of simplifying the business planning process, raising needed cash for your business quickly, and saving money on business plan preparation. Includes sections on dealing with banks, government loans, and how to get OPM (Other People's Money). Contains business opportunities in the 35 largest economic markets worldwide.

ISBN 0-940673-81-9   250 pages   8½ x 11   paperbound
$19.95

The Business Planning Guide

Creating a Plan for Success in Your Own Business

By Andy Bangs. The perfect companion to the *Instant Business Plan, The Business Planning Guide* has been used by hundreds of banks, colleges, and accounting firms to guide business owners through the process of putting together a complete and effective business plan and financing proposal. The *Guide* comes complete with examples, forms and worksheets that make the planning process painless. With over 200,000 copies in print, the *Guide* has become a small business classic.

ISBN 0-936894-96-2   208 pages   8½ x 11   paperbound
$24.95

Free Help from Uncle Sam to Start Your Own Business

(Or Expand the One You Have)
4th Edition, Completely Revised

By William Alarid and Gustav Berle. *Free Help* describes over 100 government programs that help small business and gives dozens of examples of how others have used this aid. Included are appendices with helpful books, organizations and phone numbers.

ISBN 0-940673-66-5   304 pages   5½ x 8½   paperbound
$15.95

The Instant Business Plan

Twelve Quick and Easy Steps to a Successful Business
2nd Edition

By Gustav Berle, Ph.D., and Paul Kirschner. Learn the secrets of simplifying the business planning process, raising needed cash for your business quickly, and saving money on business plan preparation. Includes sections on dealing with banks, government loans, and how to get OPM (Other People's Money).

ISBN 0-940673-88-6   200 pages   8½ x 11   paperbound
$15.95

To order by credit card from within the USA, call toll free (800) 255-5730 extension 110.

Please have Visa, MasterCard, American Express or Discover card ready.

To order by credit card from outside the USA,
please fax your credit card number, date of expiration and name on card to **(805) 925-2656.**

To order by check please mail it to:
Puma Publishing, 1670 Coral Drive, Department IMP, Santa Maria, California 93454 USA.
Sales tax: Please add 7¾% for shipping to California addresses.

Shipping airmail to addresses in USA $4.00 for first book + $2.00 per additional book. Overseas airmail shipping $16.00 for first book + $4.00 per additional book.

E-MAIL: Pumapub871@aol.com

Free Help from Uncle Sam to Start Your Own Business

(Or Expand the One You Have) 3rd Edition, Completely Revised.
By William Alarid and Gustav Berle. *Free Help* describes over 100 government programs that help small business and gives dozens of examples of how others have used this aid. Included are appendices with helpful books, organizations and phone numbers.
ISBN 0-940673-54-1 304 pages 5½x8½ paperbound $13.95

Marketing Without Advertising

By Michael Phillips and Salli Rasberry. A creative and practical guide that shows small business people how to avoid wasting money on advertising. The authors, experienced business consultants, show how to implement an ongoing marketing plan to tell potential and current customers that yours is a quality business worth trusting, recommending, and coming back to.
ISBN 0-87337-019-8 200 pages 8½x11 paperbound $13.95

The Partnership Book

By attorneys Dennis Clifford and Ralph Warner. When two or more people join to start a small business, one of the most basic needs is to establish a solid, legal partnership agreement. This book supplies a number of sample agreements which you can use as is. Buy-out clauses, unequal sharing of assets, and limited partnerships are all discussed in detail.
ISBN 0-87337-141-0 221 pages 8½x11 paperbound $24.95

The Legal Guide for Starting & Running a Small Business

By attorney Fred S. Steingold. 1st edition. What every business owner needs to know to establish and run a small business. Topics included are deciding whether to form a sole proprietorship, partnership or corporation, buying a franchise or existing business, negotiating a favorable lease, hiring and firing employees, working with independent contractors, creating good contracts and resolving business disputes.
ISBN 0-87337-174-7 400 pages 8½x11 paperbound $22.95

Small Business Law

By attorney Ralph Warner with Joanne Greene. 1st edition. Warner covers the basic legal issues facing a small business start-up: Should the potential owner organize as a sole proprietorship, partnership or corporation? What steps must be taken to protect the business name? What are the legal pitfalls in renting space, hiring employees and paying taxes?
ISBN 0-87337-210-7 50-minute audio cassette tape with 18-page booklet $14.95

The Instant Marketing Plan

Your Simple Enjoyable Easy-to-Follow Road Map to Skyrocket Your Business
By Mark Nolan. No business can survive without marketing. Here for the first time in print marketing genius Mark Nolan reveals the secrets he usually charges $400 per hour to reveal. Mark's writing style is fun and informal. You'll enjoy his experiences and you formulate a knock-out plan to bring customers to your door and have them come back again and again.
ISBN 0-940673-74-6 200 pages 8½x11 paperbound $15.95

To order by credit card, call toll-free (800) 255-5730 extension 110.

Please have Visa, MasterCard, American Express or Discover card ready, or send a check to *Puma Publishing, 1670 Coral Drive, Department IBP, Santa Maria, California 93454.* Sales Tax: Please add 7¾% for shipping to California addresses. Shipping $2.00 per book; airmail $4.00 per book. Other inquiries please FAX (805) 925-2656.

Free!

We've recently compiled a roster of state agencies that provide financial assistance to help you expand your business. This can help you to get your new marketing program off to a good start. State agencies are often much easier for you to deal with than banks, the federal government, and/or individual investors.
If you'll photocopy the form below and mail or fax it to

Puma Publishing • 1670 Coral Drive • Santa Maria • California • 93454 • USA
fax: 805-925-2656

we'll promptly send you a current copy.

Yes! Please send me your free roster of state financial assistance agencies.

Your name:_____ Your street or POB address:_____

City: _____ State or Province:_____ Zip: _____ Country: _____

Phone #: _____ Fax #: _____ e-mail address: _____

Where did you first discover *The Instant Marketing Plan?*_____

What did you like best about this book? _____

_____

_____

How would you like to see this book improved? _____

_____

_____

(Optional) My business is: _____

Other Comments: _____

_____

_____

_____